Samurai

and the Culture
of Japan's
Great Peace

Dear Eli —
We hope you enjoy
this book and bring peace
to yourself and everyone
through your interest in Samurai
culture. I would like to read
it with you! Fascinating!!
Congratulations on your
achievements, too!

Love,
grandma Jane &
grandpa Bob
1·17·20

Samurai

and the Culture of Japan's Great Peace

Fabian Drixler

William D. Fleming

Robert George Wheeler

Peabody Museum of Natural History
Yale University
New Haven, Connecticut

Distributed by Yale University Press
NEW HAVEN AND LONDON

Yale

Samurai and the Culture of Japan's Great Peace

An exhibition at the Peabody Museum of Natural History, Yale University
March 28, 2015 through January 3, 2016

Support for the exhibition was generously provided by Connecticut Humanities,
the Council on East Asian Studies at Yale University, the E. Rhodes and Leona B. Carpenter Foundation,
and The Japan Foundation, New York.

Support for this book has been provided by the O. C. Marsh Fellows Program
at the Yale Peabody Museum of Natural History.

Editors
Richard A. Kissel, *Director of Public Programs*
Rosemary Volpe, *Publications Manager*

Catalog design
Sally H. Pallatto

Exhibition design
Laura Friedman

Primary photography
William Guth

Additional photography
William K. Sacco

Collections and content support
Roger H. Colten, *Senior Collections Manager, Anthropology*

Curatorial consultants
Dani Botsman and Morgan Pitelka

Published by Peabody Museum of Natural History, Yale University
P. O. Box 208118, New Haven CT 06520-8118 USA | http://peabody.yale.edu

Distributed by Yale University Press
New Haven and London | www.yalebooks.com

ISBN 978-1-933789-03-3
Printed in the U.S.A.

Library of Congress Control Number: 2015933922

This paper meets the requirements of ANSI /NISO Z39.48-1992 (Permanence of Paper).

10 9 8 7 6 5 4 3 2 1

Contents

Director's Foreword

The Anthropology collections are critical elements of the Yale Peabody Museum's holdings, which collectively include more than 13 million objects across its 10 divisions. Carefully developed and stewarded for nearly a century and a half by generations of faculty, staff, and students, these objects are critical for understanding our world, documenting our past, and considering our future.

The Museum's Japanese collection includes a varied selection of nearly 2,000 objects, very few of which have previously seen public exhibition. With *Samurai and the Culture of Japan's Great Peace*, we are excited to share more than 150 of these stunning artifacts to tell the story of Japan's elite warriors—the samurai—from the incessant warring of their first centuries to the Great Peace of the Tokugawa period. By focusing on the Great Peace, the exhibition invites us to view the samurai in a less considered light—as agents in an increasingly complex governing structure, in which art and power were intertwined. Placing the samurai in the context of Japanese daily life, it is our hope that the exhibition will provide a deeper understanding of the samurai and their role in society.

The exhibition also highlights little known but fascinating aspects of the history of the Museum's collections, beginning with its first director O. C. Marsh and including a series of extraordinary collectors. We are also excited to include objects from the Yale University Art Gallery, Sterling Memorial Library, and the Yale Collection of Musical Instruments. We are grateful for the support and cooperation of these partners in creating a rich exhibition of objects that collectively tell a fuller story of the samurai and their world.

Our project team also represents a wonderful collaboration of talents from across the University, including Yale historians, anthropologists, collections managers, educators, and exhibition developers. In particular, I would like to express my gratitude to Fabian Drixler, William D. Fleming, and Robert George Wheeler. Their tireless efforts to develop the content for the exhibition and to author this publication are deeply appreciated. They have created a fantastic experience for our visitors. With this catalog, we bring that experience to you, and we hope you enjoy exploring the history of the samurai as told through Yale's collections.

David Skelly
Director, Peabody Museum of Natural History, Yale University
Professor of Ecology, Yale School of Forestry & Environmental Studies

Foreword

Samurai and the Culture of Japan's Great Peace is the culmination of interrelated undertakings that span more than a century, beginning with the collectors who in the late 19th and early 20th centuries acquired the artifacts now housed in the anthropology collections of the Yale Peabody Museum, and continuing through 21st-century technical analyses of the materials and techniques embodied by these objects. The early stories of this history, described in the essay on the Yale collectors by Robert George Wheeler and William Fleming, give glimpses into the colorful lives of collectors whose activities linked Yale and the origins of the Peabody Museum of Natural History with Japan at a time of great change for that nation.

The later part of the story dates to January 2003, when Dr. Wheeler, an applied physicist retired from teaching at Yale, contacted the Museum's anthropology division in search of Japanese tea ceremony objects for a seminar he was auditing in Yale's Department of the History of Art. Wheeler, a long-time student of Japanese material culture, was familiar with the Peabody's collections and knew that suitable artifacts might be available from the Museum. Over several months we reviewed most of the Museum's Japanese collections and a sampling of Chinese artifacts. Among the great discoveries that resulted from this effort were the large lacquer covered bowl and the "sea urchin" samurai helmet featured prominently in the exhibition.

We also realized that the Museum's collections contained 20 Japanese swords. Wheeler invited Morihiro Ogawa, Special Consultant for Japanese Arms and Armor at the Metropolitan Museum of Art, to New Haven to examine the swords and suits of armor. Ogawa determined that several swords were of some antiquity and worthy of restoration. Support from the E. Rhodes and Leona B. Carpenter Foundation allowed us to send five of the swords to Japan, to be worked on by Okisato Fujishiro, one of the world's premiere restorers of samurai swords.

When the restored swords returned in 2013 there was great interest among the Museum's staff in developing an exhibition of the Japanese material and planning began in earnest. Awareness of the Peabody's Japanese collections had spread in the Yale community, largely due to Wheeler's efforts. After Fabian Drixler brought his Yale class in Japanese history to the anthropology collections to see some of the objects, the exhibition team was assembled. Drixler asked Fleming, a scholar of Japanese theater and literature at Yale, to join the curatorial team. They have described the rich and complex historical and cultural context of the samurai and early Japan, bringing this side of the samurai story to museum visitors and, through this catalog, to a wider audience. This book documents both the exhibition and important objects from the Yale Peabody Museum's Japanese collections, many of which have never before been displayed or published.

On behalf of the Division of Anthropology, I would like to express our delight with *Samurai and the Culture of Japan's Great Peace.*

Roger H. Colten, *Senior Collections Manager*
Division of Anthropology, Yale Peabody Museum of Natural History

1

Samurai and the Culture of Japan's Great Peace

Today, "samurai" is a global brand: the man of uncompromising honor and loyalty, perfectly trained in the martial arts, and calmly indifferent in the face of death. But the real history of the samurai is far more complex and interesting, full of drama, transformation, and paradox.

The first samurai were the poor relations of sophisticated aristocrats, tasked to do their dirty work in the provinces. Over the centuries, they emerged as masters of the Japanese state, but by 1550 they had nearly trampled it out of existence in their unceasing battles. Within the following two generations, a new order emerged as one warlord, Tokugawa Ieyasu, succeeded in forcing all the others to recognize him as their master. During centuries when war remained a fact of daily life in the rest of the world, Japan enjoyed 250 years of uninterrupted peace (1615–1863) under the rule of Ieyasu and his descendants.

This catalog is a history in objects. Most of these objects date from the Tokugawa period, an age that those who experienced it often called "the Great Peace." Even those artifacts that appear to be functional armor or weapons were in many cases created not to protect their samurai owner or to fell his foes, but to justify his inherited power and privilege. A storied blade or an impressive suit of armor, displayed prominently in an alcove, could remind guests of the pedigree of their host. Likewise, when a samurai woman was married, her gold-dusted lacquer trousseau might include seemingly useful items such as make-up sets and writing boxes. But many of these things would have been used only rarely. Instead, they were designed to remind the bride's new household of the wealth and rank of her native family. In a sense, being exhibited was the original purpose of many of the artifacts in the exhibition.

During the Great Peace, the samurai constituted only about five percent of Japan's population. In the pages that follow, the worlds of the other 95 percent come to life as well: men and women fearful of samurai violence but swept up in the romance of samurai loyalty, vengeance, and honor; people living and dying according to ideals that alternately strike us as familiar and alien; subjects forbidden to leave Japanese shores, but intensely curious about the world beyond.

The objects in this catalog came to New Haven by a variety of routes. Some of the exquisite pieces of Japanese lacquerware were purchased from Ainu owners in Hokkaido in August of 1896. The Ainu, a people living in small-scale communities on the islands north of Honshu, had a distinctive and creative material culture of their own, but they also eagerly collected Japanese objects as markers of wealth and for ceremonial use. In one sense, the Ainu, exploited and marginalized, were a world away from the globetrotting American collectors to whom they sold some of their possessions. Yet in the way they related to the material culture of Tokugawa Japan, they also shared surprising commonalities with their American visitors—and with us, who read our own meanings into these artifacts.

Opposite:
1 Samurai helmet and armor (Late 18th to mid-19th century, in the style of the 13th to 14th century, documented repairs in 1855)

This suit of armor dates from around 1800, but is similar in style to what samurai would have worn about 400 years earlier. Why would its original owner, the territorial lord (*daimyo*) of Okazaki, have paid good money for armor four centuries behind the times?

Archaic-revival armor of this kind signaled that this was a house with a great pedigree, proud of its illustrious ancestors. Another reason is that, by 1800, the states of Japan had been at peace for nearly two centuries. Samurai took their armor out of its boxes to display it in an alcove or for use in the occasional parade or maneuver.

2

Before the Great Peace

A thousand years ago, Japan was ruled by an imperial court that measured a man's worth by his lineage and the panache of his poetry. Shedding blood was a horror, a dangerous form of spiritual pollution.

For centuries, a caste of hereditary warriors guarded this order by hunting down bandits and defeating the enemies of the court. These armed servants were known in Japanese by several names, including *mononofu, tsuwamono, bushi*—and *samurai*. In fact, the word *samurai* means "one who serves."

Over subsequent generations, the power of these martial "servants" grew, while that of their courtly masters waned. Conflicts in the formerly tranquil capital of Heian-kyō (now Kyoto) came to be settled by force of arms; in the outlying provinces, warriors claimed an increasing share of the harvest. Central authority strengthened in some generations and weakened in others. But over the centuries, the very existence of the center was jeopardized.

By about 1550, the samurai had nearly trampled the old order out of existence. As warlords fought each other in the provinces, the once-sprawling ancient capital had shrunk to two fortified neighborhoods. The emperor in his threadbare palace had become so poor that he depended on gifts of rice balls from a loyal confectioner for his breakfasts.

Opposite:
2 Detail from
a folding screen
Scene from
the Battle of Yashima
(Mid-17th century)

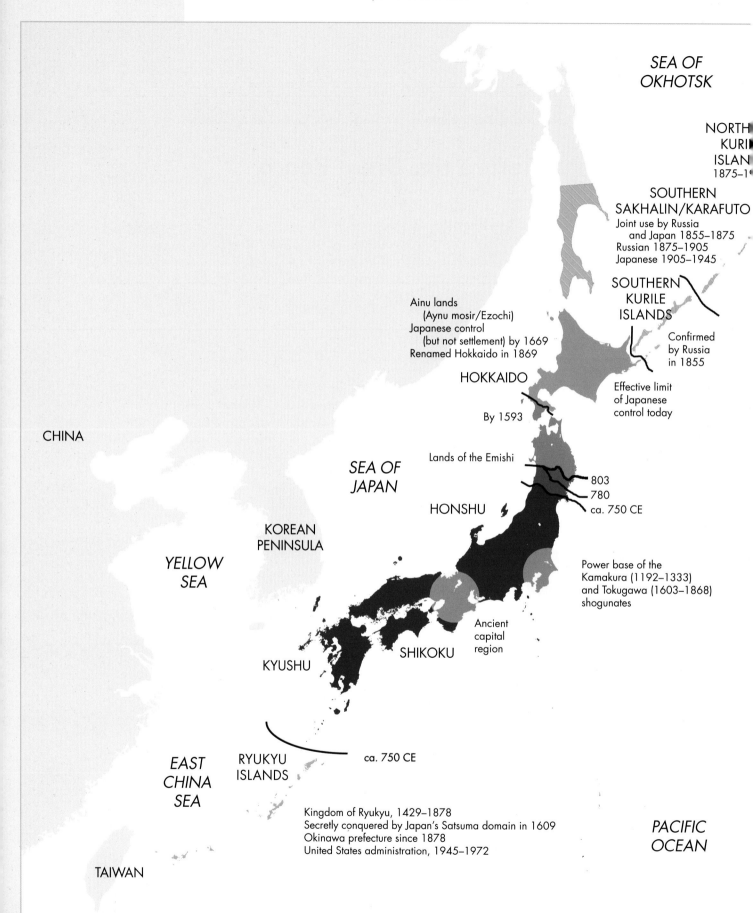

SEA OF
OKHOTSK

NORTH
KURI
ISLAN
1875–1

SOUTHERN
SAKHALIN/KARAFUTO
Joint use by Russia
and Japan 1855–1875
Russian 1875–1905
Japanese 1905–1945

SOUTHERN
KURILE
ISLANDS

Confirmed
by Russia
in 1855

Ainu lands
(Aynu mosir/Ezochi)
Japanese control
(but not settlement) by 1669
Renamed Hokkaido in 1869

Effective limit
of Japanese
control today

HOKKAIDO

By 1593

CHINA

Lands of the Emishi

803
780
ca. 750 CE

SEA OF
JAPAN

HONSHU

KOREAN
PENINSULA

YELLOW
SEA

Power base of the
Kamakura (1192–1333)
and Tokugawa (1603–1868)
shogunates

Ancient
capital
region

SHIKOKU

KYUSHU

EAST
CHINA
SEA

RYUKYU
ISLANDS

ca. 750 CE

Kingdom of Ryukyu, 1429–1878
Secretly conquered by Japan's Satsuma domain in 1609
Okinawa prefecture since 1878
United States administration, 1945–1972

PACIFIC
OCEAN

TAIWAN

BERING
SEA

3

The Islands of Japan

Japan's territory is only as large as the state of Montana but stretches from the subtropics to the subarctic. Mountains are never far away, and the plains, once full of marshes and lakes, today host almost all of Japan's agriculture, as well as several of the world's great cities.

Modern Japan comprises four main islands and the Ryukyu archipelago in the south. But these boundaries have changed over time. Before the late 16th century, not even all of the main island of Honshu was fully integrated into the Japanese state. The northern island of Hokkaido acquired this status only in the 1870s, and Ryukyu—also known as Okinawa—was a formally independent kingdom until 1878.

The samurai originated at the very edges of Japan. Around 800 CE, the imperial court in Heian-kyō sent its conscript armies to subdue the indomitable inhabitants of northern Honshu, known as the Emishi ("Shrimp Barbarians"). There they faced mounted archers of lethal skill. In the words of one chronicle: "Horse-and-bow warfare is learned from birth by the barbarians. Ten of our subjects cannot equal one of them." Eventually the generals began to learn from their foes. Rather than conscripts forcibly drafted from their farms, professional fighters trained from boyhood in horsemanship and archery came to form the backbone of the court's army.

© FABIAN DRIXLER

4   Samurai blade
(15th century)
Signed, Yamato no kuni jūnin
Kanesuke (大和國住人包助)

Mounted warriors galloped across Japan from at least 500 CE, but contact with the Emishi of northern Honshu remolded them about three centuries later. In ancient Japan, swords were straight and short, with two sharp edges. The first known examples of curved slashing swords—the ancestors of the samurai sword—come from the Emishi.

5 Folding screen
Scene from
the Battle of Yashima
(Mid-17th century)

The Battle of Yashima

In the early 1180s—a time of volcanic eruptions, harvest failures, and upheaval around the world—two great samurai clans, the Heike (also known as Taira) and the Minamoto (Genji), fought a five-year war. This screen shows a scene from their penultimate battle.

The clash between the Minamoto and the Heike has sometimes been understood as a war between Eastern Japan—a land of horse-breeders—and Western Japan, whose many isles and inlets were easier to control with fast ships. In the spring of 1185, the Heike abandoned the capital of Heian-kyō and retreated to a coastal fortress farther to the west. When the Minamoto attacked, the Heike took to their ships.

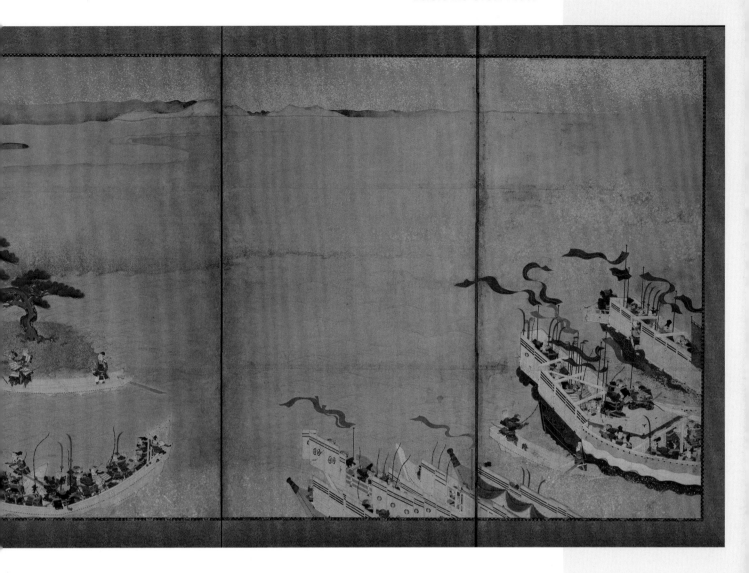

In this screen, we see the mounted archers under the white Minamoto banner, while the fleet flies the Heike red. A Heike archer, standing on the small boat beneath the pine tree at center, has loosed a shaft at the enemy commander, Minamoto no Yoshitsune, who is seated astride a black charger in the middle of the second panel. One of Yoshitsune's men takes the arrow instead, and falls headlong to the ground.

The Tale of the Heike, the great epic inspired by the Heike-Minamoto war, gives this fallen man a heroic final speech: "I regret only that I must die without seeing my lord rise to prominence. … For a warrior to have it told in later generations that he exchanged his life for his master's—that is an honor in this world and a memory for the next."

That the artist painted this scene in the 17th century suggests that even centuries later this samurai ideal still resonated powerfully.

*7   The Sea Bed at Daimotsu Bay
Danmotsu no ura kaitei no zu
(1851)*

*6   "Samurai" crab
Paradorippe granulata*

Souls of the Vanquished

When Japanese fishermen pulled up crabs like this one, they saw an angry samurai face on the shell's surface and thought of the restless spirits of drowned warriors. The Heike-Minamoto war ended in 1185 in a great sea battle. As the Heike cause was lost, even the boy emperor, grandson of a maternal Heike grandfather, plunged to a watery grave.

In Japan, the souls of those slain in battle have long been feared by the living. *The Tale of the Heike* was itself chanted in part to calm and honor the souls of the fallen.

The word *heike-gani* ("Heike crab") appears as early as 1638. In 1851 it inspired the woodblock artist Utagawa Kuniyoshi. In his depiction above, the Heike dead gather as ghosts at the bottom of the sea, still bleeding from their battle wounds. Of their sunken fleet, only a shell-encrusted anchor remains. Some of the warriors have metamorphosed into crabs, marching off as if to attack their old foes.

For several decades, crabs with carapaces bearing the angry-face pattern have been held up as an example of man-made evolution. Fishermen, it was said, would throw back the "samurai crabs" and eat only those without the humanoid features, until eventually all of the crabs bore the angry samurai face. It is a good story, but not true. Species that consistently have similar grooves exist in other parts of the world and appear in the fossil record long before humans.

8   Lord Minamoto no
Yoritomo's Hunt at the
Foot of Mount Fuji
Minamoto no Yoritomo kō Fuji
no susono makigari no zu,
sanmai tsuzuki
(1810s)

The Shogun's Great Hunt

Eight years had passed since the watery defeat of the Heike. In 1193, the victor, Minamoto no Yoritomo, called together his leading vassals from across Japan to a series of hunts near his power base in the country's east. The grandest of these began early that summer. For an entire month, the hunt roamed across the foothills of Japan's tallest and most beautiful peak, Mount Fuji.

Minamoto no Yoritomo is the rider under the umbrella, wearing a courtly cap and a *hitatare* robe, the formal hunting dress of the samurai. At the time, he had just received the title of Seii taishōgun— "Great General Who Subdues the Eastern Barbarians"—or *shogun* for short. Except for a short gap in the late 16th century, shogun remained the title of the titular leader of Japan's samurai until 1868.

One day at dusk, a huge boar charged at Yoritomo. We see the beast as it tosses one samurai in the air and tramples another. As Yoritomo's bodyguards form a defensive circle around their liege, one man, Nitta Tadatsune, stands barehanded in the boar's path, about to win lasting fame.

Many historians see the hunt of 1193 as a grand spectacle in which Yoritomo asserted his authority. It has also been argued that the ceremony and political symbolism of the hunt point to the origins of the samurai at the edges of Japan's agricultural mainstream civilization.

The print itself is from the 1810s, much closer in time to us than to the events it depicts. Six centuries after Yoritomo, however, shoguns still conducted great hunts as military exercises and demonstrations of power. Even to this day, the great hunt of 1193 is celebrated in festivals in several parts of Japan.

9a, 9b, 9c Three images illustrating the Ikkō Ikki victory over Togashi Masachika. *An Illustrated Biography of Oda Nobunaga Ehon shūi Shinchōki* (1803)

Armed Leagues and Warrior Monks

As samurai fought unending wars in the mid-1400s, farmers and townspeople created armed leagues (*ikki*) to defend themselves. Some of these formed around temples. One of the greatest moments of such a league is shown in this sequence of three illustrations. In 1488, the Honganji temple league (*Ikkō Ikki*) allied with samurai to field an enormous army against the warlord ruling Kaga province.

Compare this army with the small aristocratic force on the folding screen from the Heike-Minamoto War. We see a dense crowd of foot soldiers, most of them commoners assembling under banners that read "Homage to Amida, the Buddha of Infinite Light." They beat drums, ring bells, and blow conch shells. The artist seems to be saying "Imagine the din!" In the foreground, we also see some of their professional allies, samurai in expensive armor.

The temple league swept aside the warlord's army, stormed his castle, and drove him to suicide. For the next century, Buddhist priests and their warrior monks and armed laymen ruled Kaga province, as well as many neighboring areas. In Kyoto, too, armed temple leagues formed by townspeople were often the strongest military force. Could Japan have developed into a Buddhist theocracy like Tibet? In the end, it did not. The samurai regained the upper hand and in the 1560s and 1570s a series of wars, massacres, and sieges broke the power of armed Buddhism.

These illustrations were made more than 300 years after the events, and are not correct in every detail. Guns only became prominent in Japanese warfare in the mid-16th century, as did the type of castle shown here.

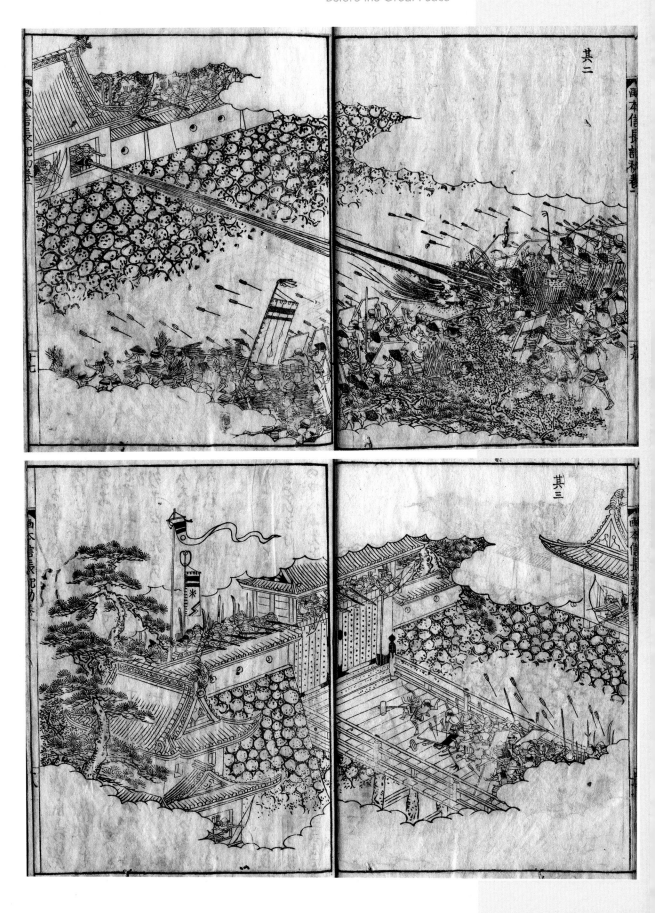

10   Kawabata Dōki,
a Kyoto confectioner, brings
the emperor his breakfast
Detail from *Ie no kagami*,
a painted family history
of Kawabata Dōki
(Tokugawa period)

Opposite:
*11   Samurai helmet
and face guard
(16th century)*

In the Western tradition, doves
are a symbol of peace. In
Japan, pigeons were sacred
to Hachiman, the god of
warriors. This helmet likely
dates from the 16th century.
During this time of ever-larger
battles, rapidly growing
firepower, decade-long sieges,
and even a Japanese attempt
to conquer Korea and China,
Hachiman must have received
many prayers.

The iron bowl (*hachi*) of this
helmet is made from 16 plates,
assembled by standing iron
rivets backed by iron washers.
The rivets gradually decrease
in size toward the crown,
minimizing weight. In general,
the bowl shape of samurai
helmets changed in the 15th
to 16th centuries from nearly
hemispherical to an elongated
design, allowing greater
comfort with a thick liner and
improved impact protection.

The Emperor's Breakfast

Japan's imperial line survived these centuries of war and chaos,
but only barely. In the 16th century it was impoverished. One
faithful confectioner took pity on the emperor's plight and began
carrying gifts of food to the crumbling palace. By the 1560s, this
gift had become a ritual: every morning the townsman brought
the emperor a simple breakfast of six rice cakes covered in salted
bean paste.

Imagine the emperor consuming such plain food under a leaky
roof, while in the provinces warlords reached for the sky in their
newly built castles.

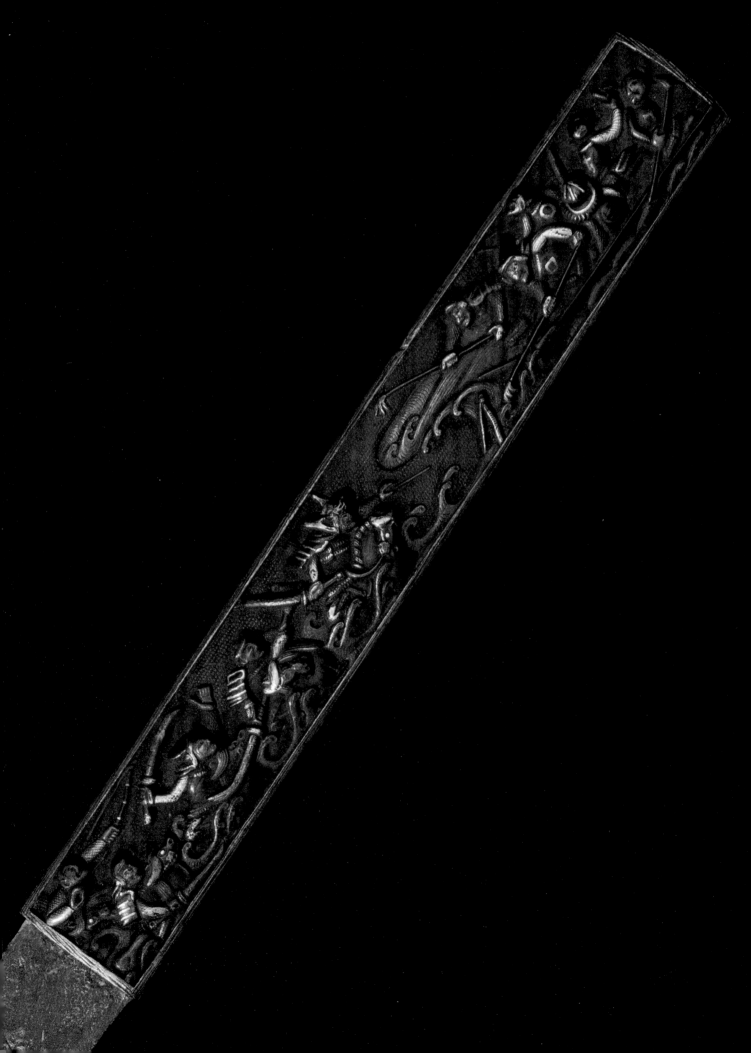

3

The Art and Science of the Sword

As a weapon, the samurai sword was not all that important. Bows, spears, and (from the 1550s) guns decided most battles. What set the sword apart from other arms was the beauty and mystery of its craftsmanship.

Samurai had begun to fetishize the sword even as they still fought wars. In 1583, one Italian visitor to Japan noted that his host had paid 4,500 ducats for a single famous sword—16 times its weight in gold!

Ironically, the cult of the sword only grew more intense during the Great Peace. Samurai alone now had the right to bear them in public, and it was indeed their duty to do so. Great lords (*daimyo*) underscored their power and pedigree by collecting the finest blades, to be exchanged as gifts or put on display. In this sense, samurai swords were museum pieces long before the first American museum opened its doors.

Most American samurai exhibitions uncritically perpetuate the portrait that daimyo families have liked to paint of themselves through their collections: as perfect warrior-gentlemen, deadly in combat but refined in their artistic tastes.

To understand the hold of the samurai sword on the Japanese and global imagination alike, we too emphasize their beauty and explain how they were forged. But as you admire their mirror surfaces, we invite you to look past the image the swords were meant to project. Think instead of a daimyo justifying his inherited wealth and power by displaying a sword as a storied work of art, or of commoners giving a wide berth to samurai on the street. In more ways than one, swords were a tool of domination in a hierarchical caste society.

Opposite:
12 Detail showing what is probably a scene from the Battle of Yashima on the knife of a short sword scabbard (Late 18th to early 19th century)

What Could a Samurai Do with His Sword?

While wars were still fought, he could carry it into battle. But with arrows, pikes, and muskets also used, he might never take it from its scabbard.

The rest of the time, he could display it on a rack in his home. If it was a fine blade, and perhaps a storied one, he could impress visitors with his family's history and rank.

When walking the street, his two swords—one long, one short—were an immediate, obvious signal of samurai status.

He could give his sword away as a gift. A beautiful sword offered to a superior at just the right time could expunge an offense or scandal, thereby saving the giver's position and livelihood.

If a samurai's father or brother had been murdered by another samurai, he could apply to the authorities for permission to carry out revenge.

He could also use his sword to strike down a disrespectful commoner. This did not happen very often, in part because samurai had to prove afterward that the commoner had indeed been insolent.

Top:
13 Short sword blade
(17th to 18th century)
Signed, Hōshū-jū Fujiwara
Masayuki (豊州住藤原正行)

14 Long sword blade
(15th century)
Unsigned

Bottom:
15 Long sword scabbard
(18th to 19th century)

16 Short sword scabbard
(Late 18th to early 19th century)

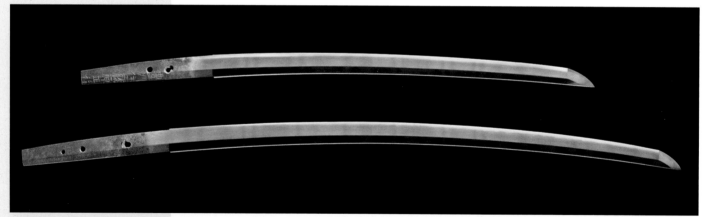

Forging a Samurai Blade

Samurai swords are among the sharpest and toughest in the world. In an ode to a Japanese sword, the 11th-century Chinese poet Ouyang Xiu reported the popular opinion that blades from Japan could "cut through jade." In the 17th century, the Dutch writer Arnoldus Montanus thought them "so well wrought, and exceedingly temper'd, that they will cut our European blades asunder."

Even though these claims were exaggerated, there is no question that Japanese swords are astonishing feats of engineering. Smiths perfected their properties many centuries before anyone understood the science of why some kinds of steel are sharper or tougher than others. The samurai sword is a monument to what humans can achieve empirically, through trial and error.

Top:
18 Short sword blade
(Mid-19th century)
Signed, Ōshū-jū Nagamichi
(奥州住長道), dated 1861

19 Long sword blade
(16th century)
Signed, Bishū Osafune Suke
Sada (備州長舩祐定)

Bottom:
20 Short sword scabbard
(19th century)

21 Long sword scabbard
(Late 18th to early 19th century)

17 Sword calamity amulet

The presence of samurai must have been uncomfortable for many commoners. Some carried amulets like this one to protect themselves from "sword calamities"—that is, being cut down by a samurai. Most swords, then, were used not as weapons of war, but as decoration, as markers of status in a caste society, and as a means of instilling fear in the 95 percent of Japanese who were not samurai.

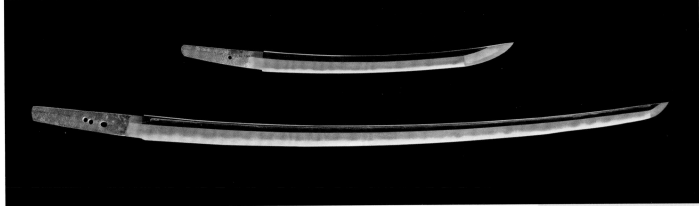

*22 The Swordsmith
of Mount Inari
Inari-yama kokaji
(1887)
From Gekkō's Miscellany
Gekkō zuihitsu
(1886–1887)*

According to a legend dramatized in the noh play *The Swordsmith*, Emperor Ichijō (reigned 986–1011) had an auspicious dream and was inspired to have a smith forge him a sword. Worried that his abilities were not sufficient, the swordsmith prayed for assistance to the god Inari, who appeared before him and aided him in the task. Gekkō's print shows the smith and Inari alternating blows to the blade, with Inari accompanied by the white foxes that serve as his divine messengers. To honor the god, the sword itself was given the name Little Fox (Kogitsune-maru).

From Sand to Sword: The Science Behind the Blade

The steel for a sword is produced by smelting iron ore sand with charcoal to form an alloy of iron containing 1.3 to 1.5 percent carbon. Since the best steel for swords has slightly less than 0.8 percent carbon, the smith burns off some of the carbon during the repeated folding and forging of the alloy at high temperatures in air.

With this carbon content, the crystal structure of the iron atoms in steel at a temperature above about 740 °C (about 1400 °F) is *face-centered cubic*. If cooled quickly the alloy retains its face-centered cubic structure, and face-centered cubic steel is very hard, but brittle. But if cooled more slowly, liberating large amounts of heat energy, a transition to *body-centered cubic* occurs. This steel is strong, ductile, and flexible.

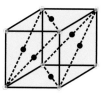
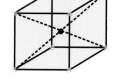

Face-centered cubic   Body-centered cubic

The Japanese swordsmiths learned these facts empirically, for we see these two types of steel in their swords. On forging the sword shapes, they covered the thick side of the blade with clay but left the cutting edge exposed. Smiths heated the combination to above 740 °C, a temperature they gauged through the color of the heated metal, and then quenched the blade in water. The exposed part is quickly cooled, making it very hard. The protected thick side cooled slowly because of the thermal insulating properties of the clay. The wavy pattern that extends down the length of the blade—the *hamon* ("wave pattern")—represents the boundary between the face-centered cubic and body-centered cubic crystal structures.

The differential cooling also contributes to the distinctive curvature of samurai swords. The blade is further shaped after forging, and is then polished in several stages. Some blades were signed by their maker on the tang, the end of the blade that is covered by the handle.

Through this process, Japanese swordsmiths overcame the basic tradeoff between toughness and sharpness, creating a strong flexible blade with a very hard edge.

Restoring the Peabody's Swords

Five blades from the Yale Peabody Museum's collection were recently restored by Myōga Akiko and Fujishiro Okisato, one of Japan's premier sword-polishers and a "National Living Treasure." The swords' scabbards were also restored in Japan by Kawanobe Tomoaki, and some of the handles were repaired by Okabe Hisao.

The Museum gratefully acknowledges the E. Rhodes and Leona B. Carpenter Foundation for its support of this restoration.

The Beauty of Blades

The place where the harder steel of the blade's edge meets the softer, more supple steel of its center and back emerges as a misty swirl after polishing. This swirl (*hamon*) is one of the features connoisseurs admire in individual swords.

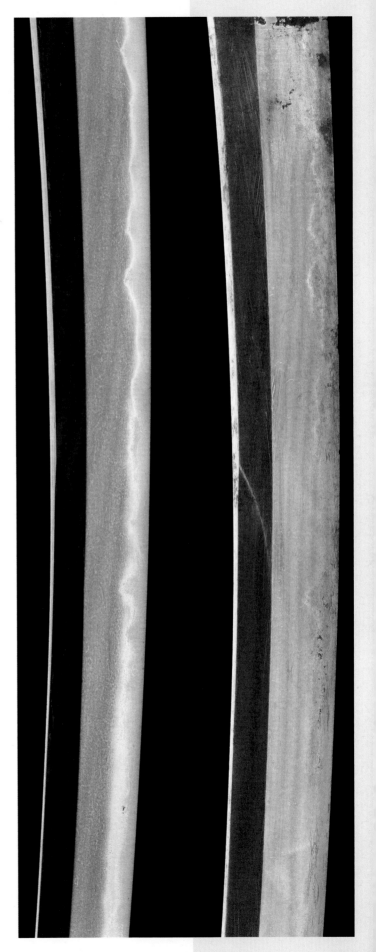

23 Short sword blade before (right) and after (left) restoration
(19th century)
Inscribed Ōshū-jū Nagamichi
(奥州住長道), dated 1861

4

Edo and the Architecture of the Great Peace

The incessant wars of the "Warring States" period (1467–1590) came to an end with the hegemony of one warlord, Toyotomi Hideyoshi. When he died in 1598, his son and heir Hideyori was only five years old. The regency council sworn to protect him soon fell apart, its members forming two armed coalitions. In 1600, they faced each other at Sekigahara, a battle whose scale and round date has given it watershed status in Japanese history. The victor, Tokugawa Ieyasu, was a man of Hideyoshi's own generation. In the aftermath of Sekigahara, some of Ieyasu's enemies lost their heads or their lands, and many others became his vassals. In 1603, he acquired the title of shogun. Two years later, he passed the title on to his adult son, thus securing the succession. In 1614, Ieyasu used a pretext to attack Hideyori, now a young man and still in many eyes the legitimate ruler of Japan. The following year, as Tokugawa samurai swarmed across the ramparts of his castle, Hideyori took his own life.

From this ominous beginning the Tokugawa shoguns achieved something remarkable: 250 years of peace (1615 to 1863) for the 250 small states that made up their island realm. Tokugawa Ieyasu, the founder of the line, initially built that peace on his mastery of violence on a grand scale. Ieyasu's life was unusually lucky and unusually long. He fought his first battle at the age of 15 and his last at 72, a year before his death in 1616. In that last battle, he commanded an army of about 200,000 men at a time when 30,000 soldiers was the largest force any European ruler could assemble in one place.

The Great Peace of the Tokugawa shogunate balanced rigorous central controls with local autonomy. By the reign of Ieyasu's grandson, all local lords (*daimyo*) were required to spend half their time in Edo—comfortable hostages in the shadow of the shogun's great castle. All marriages between daimyo families required the approval of the shogun, as did even small repairs to fortifications. The slightest breach of these rules could cost a lord his land and titles. Even without provocation, the shoguns ordered many daimyo to move their castles from one end of Japan to the other.

But the daimyo, too, derived great benefits from the Tokugawa settlement. For the first time, they enjoyed security of tenure, safe from plotting underlings or conquest by aggressive neighbors. In the Warring States period, warlords had to fight and seize new lands if they wanted to survive. In the new paradigm of the Great Peace, they were able to enjoy their status as members of Japan's most exclusive club.

The power of the shogunate often looked greater on paper than it was in practice. Officially, all daimyo were vassals of the shogun and held their lands at his pleasure. In practice, they enjoyed autonomy in governing their own states, which they treated as the property of their family. As long as daimyo acted in public as his obedient servants, the shogun allowed them to rule as small kings inside their own domains.

Opposite:
24 Lacquer food bowl (jikirō)
(Possibly early 17th century)

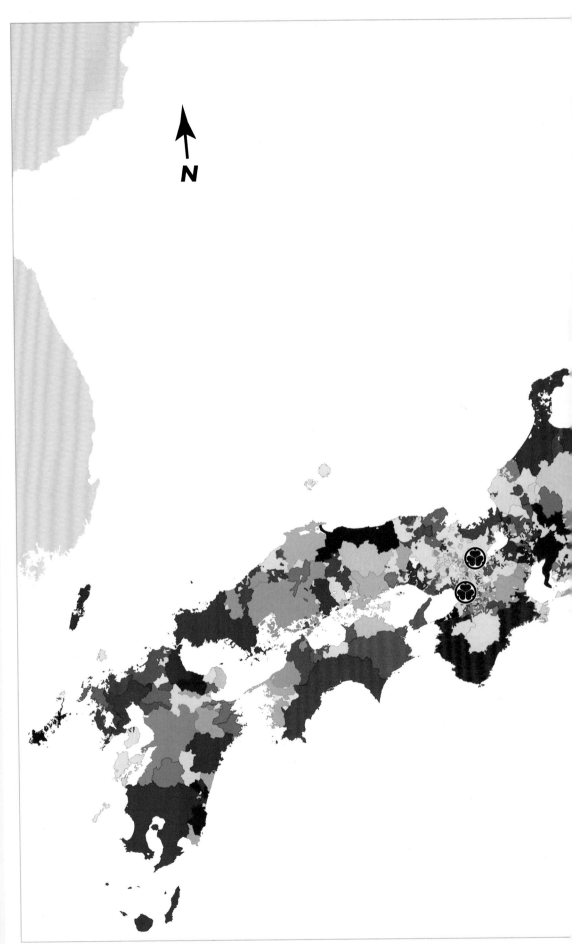

25   Each color indicates one of Japan's 227 daimyo territories in 1664. Although as accurate as possible, this map is somewhat simplified, since some of Japan's 40,000 villages were divided among 10 different daimyo!

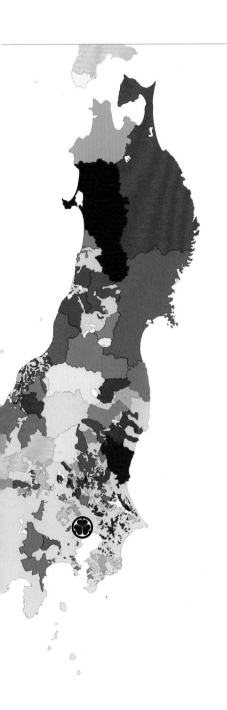

Lands of the Tokugawa Shogun

The Great Peace is even more remarkable if we think of Japan as not one country, but a collection of some 250 states and statelets. Each state had its own castle and samurai army, as well as a daimyo descended from men who had won power on the battlefield. Some of these states were no more than portfolios of widely scattered villages. But others were compact territories, called "countries" by their hundreds of thousands of inhabitants.

The Tokugawa maintained the peace not by crushing all their competitors, but by creating a system in which—for the first time in centuries—Japan's ruling elite no longer needed to fear destruction at the hands of their peers.

In the city of Kyoto, an emperor reigned throughout the Tokugawa period, exalted above all other mortals. The shoguns made sure he did not go hungry, but also kept him effectively confined in his modest yet tasteful palace.

 The great cities (from west to east) of Osaka, Kyoto, and Edo, all under direct shogunate control

 The shogun's lands

© FABIAN DRIXLER

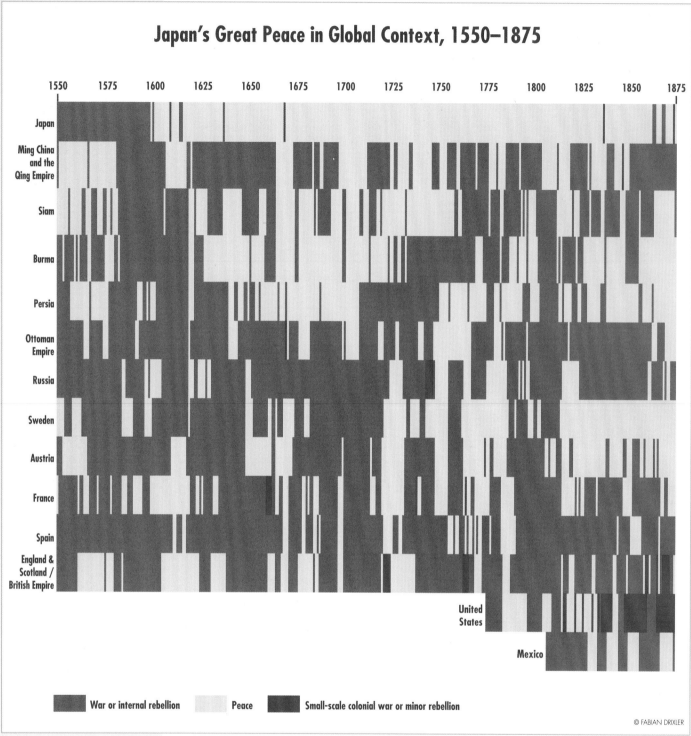

Japan's Great Peace in Global Context, 1550–1875

War or internal rebellion   Peace   Small-scale colonial war or minor rebellion

© FABIAN DRIXLER

26 The precise dividing line between "war or internal rebellion" and "small-scale colonial war or minor rebellion" is to some degree arbitrary, but serves to distinguish conflicts that posed a significant military challenge to the state in question from those that did not.

War and Peace

In the global context of its time, Japan's Great Peace was truly exceptional. In Japan, war passed from memory and into legend, but most other major states in the early modern world were at war far more often than they were at peace.

A Marriage Alliance in Lacquer and Gold

This lacquer bowl, with its striking lightning design in gold and silver, may date to the early 1600s. Its materials are precious and its workmanship exquisite, but what was its purpose?

Adorning the bowl are crests that point to two of Japan's grandest families —the Tokugawa and Mōri. At Sekigahara, the battle that made Tokugawa Ieyasu master of Japan, Mōri Terumoto was the titular commander of the opposing force, although he was so ambivalent about fighting Ieyasu that he did not himself show up on the battlefield. In the aftermath of the battle, Terumoto lost 70 percent of his lands as well as his castle at Hiroshima, but remained one of Japan's most important daimyo.

It is possible that this bowl celebrates the marriage of Tokugawa Ieyasu's (adopted) granddaughter with Mōri Terumoto's son. In this sense, it may be a monument to the carefully balanced politics of compromise that turned a dangerous enemy into a reliable vassal.

In 1896, the bowl's owner was an old Ainu woman in the northern reaches of Japan, living in a simple hut. She sold it to Mabel Loomis Todd, a Massachusetts writer who was visiting Japan with her astronomer husband.

The Ainu collected precious lacquer as status symbols and ritual objects. By the 17th century, artisans in all of Japan's major lacquer centers supplied this demand. Some artists may have added impressive-looking crests without permission to raise the price. However, it also seems that some artifacts from daimyo collections found their way to the Ainu. Many Ainu were certainly connoisseurs of the fine points of lacquerware, and would pay extra for a particularly beautiful object.

Research on the attribution of this object is ongoing.

The crests of the Tokugawa (above) and Mōri families (below). Note the discrepancy between the usual Tokugawa crest and the mon on the bowl. The combination of the triple hollyhock (*mitsuba aoi*) of the Tokugawa with the triple sword (*sanken*) of the Minamoto is highly unusual, but may reflect Ieyasu's claim to be the head of the Minamoto clan (*Genji no ōja*).

27 Lacquer food bowl (*jikirō*) (Possibly early 17th century)

25

28, 29 Folding screens
A panorama of Edo
Edo-zu byōbu
(Likely painted between
1654 and 1662)

Scenes from the Shogun's Capital

This pair of screens shows the city of Edo in the 1640s, the height of the reign of the third Tokugawa shogun, Tokugawa Iemitsu (1623–1651). Although the screens teem with poignant detail of commoner life, they show an idealized version of the shogun's city, centered on the architecture and pastimes of the samurai elite.

Shortly after the period the screens portray, Edo became what was probably the world's most populous city. Each daimyo had to maintain at least one palace in Edo and spend every other year in residence there, along with a retinue of samurai. Add in their families and servants, and the merchants and artisans who supplied their needs, and by 1700 Edo had grown to more than a million inhabitants.

What is the meaning of the golden clouds?

Golden clouds swirl across both screens. The idea is not that Edo was full of smoke or mist (although it may have been, with at least a hundred thousand hearths and frequent fires), but to allow the artist to create individual scenes showing separate moments in time in a single grand, sprawling cityscape. In one place on the screen, an urban neighborhood celebrates the New Year, while elsewhere spring blossoms billow and autumn foliage blazes.

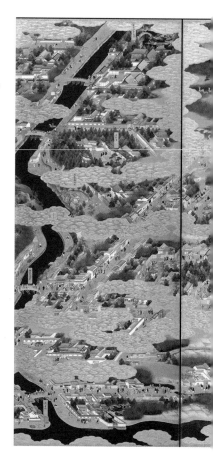

Who commissioned the screens?

There are several competing theories.

The (inverted) crest of Sakai Tadakatsu, lord of Obama, appears on the field camp (*manmaku*) enclosures. Sakai was one of Tokugawa Iemitsu's most trusted ministers.

On the golden clouds, however, there appear alternating crests of one and two butterflies. This may be a clever pun: another trusted minister of Tokugawa Iemitsu, Matsudaira Nobutsuna, had a crest of three butterflies.

Either man could have commissioned the screen to impress the shogun when receiving him in his own palace, or to commemorate Iemitsu's rule after his death. However, other analysts of the screens point to several glaring mistakes by the painter in the placement of some buildings and the architecture of the great keep of Edo castle, which burned down in 1657. They suggest that the screens were painted long after Iemitsu's death, perhaps around 1710 when the shogunate briefly considered rebuilding the keep. If true, the screens may express nostalgia for what in memory appeared to be a golden age of grand architechture and shogunal prosperity.

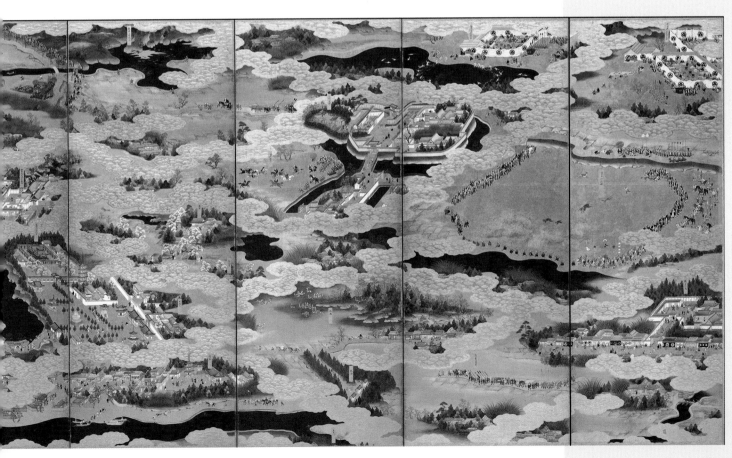

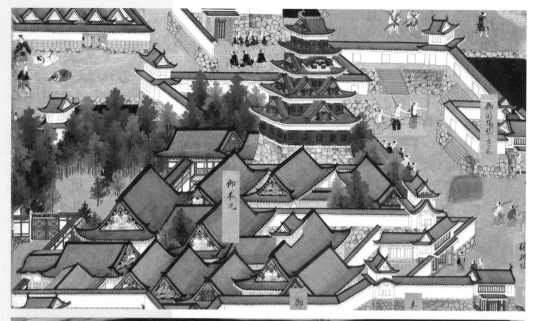

28a The great keep of Edo Castle was a seven-story structure of huge wooden pillars on a cyclopean stone pedestal. The version shown here (with some mistakes) was built in 1638 and soared 180 feet (almost 55 meters) into the sky, by far the tallest structure in Edo. But it burned down in 1657 and was never rebuilt. Japan's forests had been heavily logged by this time, and it was not easy to procure new timber of the right size and quality. Several decades into the Great Peace, it may also have seemed less critical to demonstrate the shogun's power with a great tower looming over his city.

29a Like Minamoto no Yoritomo, the first ruling shogun, the Tokugawa shoguns staged great hunts to cement ties with their vassals. Here, Tokugawa Iemitsu looks on as a deer leaps into a river to escape the lance of a samurai. An umbrella shields the shogun from our gaze. He is shown more than 20 times on this pair of screens, but his face is always hidden. This is a sign of respect. Although European monarchs liked to put their faces on coins and paintings, many Japanese rulers preferred to remain unseen, allowing distance and mystery to magnify their power.

29b Cooks prepare a great feast in a field camp. Before the late 19th century, the Japanese did not assemble around a large table for shared meals. Instead, every diner had his own lacquered tray, like the red trays carried by the two servants in black liveries. These military-style encampments enclosed by walls of cloth (*baku* or *maku*) are the origin of the Japanese name for the shogun's government: *bakufu*, or "tent government."

28b A procession of Korean ambassadors, in their distinctive horsehair hats and flowing robes, approaches the shogun's palace. For the Koreans, in light of the Japanese invasions that had devastated Korea in the 1590s, these periodic embassies were a cheap price to pay to maintain peace with their samurai neighbors. For the shogun, they were a gratifying international recognition of his status as Japan's de facto ruler. And for the Japanese at large, the Korean missions were important cultural events—Koreans were admired for their expertise in Chinese law, poetry, and medicine, and Japanese scholars vied to learn from them. A crowd of curious onlookers keeps a respectful distance from the foreign dignitaries.

28c Daimyo palaces occupied more than half the land of Edo. All had multiple gates. The most ornate of these, which in this painting is covered in lacquer and gold leaf, was reserved for the shogun's visit, even though such visits were rare; many such portals would never have been opened. The hierarchy of entryways continued from there: a gate for honored guests, then consecutively smaller and more austere entrances for the household head, family members, and servants. This palace, right across the moat of the castle, is the residence of the lord of Mito. As the 11th son of Tokugawa Ieyasu, he had a better chance than most daimyo to get to host the shogun, who was his nephew.

29c Like most daimyo, the lord of Mito maintained multiple residences in Edo. Alongside the relatively compact, formal palace near the shogun's castle, he owned a larger, leafier estate on the outskirts of the city. This lovely Japanese garden, complete with a waterfall, forms part of his "lower residence," as these sprawling compounds were known.

29

28d Two jolly samurai armies stage a mock battle, whacking each other with canes. Among the 5,000 people depicted on this screen, there is not a single samurai in full armor. Perhaps this is a faithful reflection of the streetscapes of Edo around 1650, but it is also well to remember the apparent intended message of the screens: under the shogun's wise rule, the realm is at peace.

28e In a busy downtown area, passersby admire a seasonal decoration: a miniature castle around which puppet samurai fight a battle. These Tokugawa action figures, displayed for the Boys' Festival in early summer, wear the only armor visible on these screens.

29d A group of samurai, recognizable by their swords, enjoys an outing to the countryside to admire the cherry blossoms. A servant balances lacquer boxes with food, a saké bottle, and a picnic blanket on a pole. At left, a group of women is drawn to the same beautiful spot.

28f There was no wheeled transport on the highways of Tokugawa Japan. Bulk goods were carried by boat whenever possible, and by packhorse in inland areas. Here barges unload rice, packed in bales of straw, onto the embankments of Edo's canals. Samurai received their stipends in rice. Rice was therefore brought to Edo not just as a foodstuff, but also as a kind of currency.

28g Edo was one of the most fire-prone cities in world history, with seven major conflagrations in an average year. Large quantities of timber had to be brought to the city almost continuously. But Edo's architecture cleverly made use of slender beams and posts, which could be obtained from young, faster-growing trees.

28h Nihonbashi, the bridge at the center of Edo's downtown, bustles with life. A group of *kabukimono* (masterless samurai in extravagant outfits) stands out with their colorful clothing. To their right, a Buddhist priest holds up a painted scroll and gives a sermon, but some of the pedestrians are more interested in the traffic on the canal, and lean over the railing of the bridge to watch the boats go by. Behind them, a beggar dressed in gray rags waits for alms. On the left bank, wooden signboards known as *kōsatsu* tower over a small enclosure. The shogun's laws were displayed throughout Japan on signboards like these. Several people are seen reading them intently. The artist might be implying that in a realm at peace, subjects abide by the law.

30 Evening Rain at Koizumi
Koizumi no yau
From the series
Eight Views of Kanazawa
Kanazawa hakkei
(ca. 1835–1836,
later printing)

In this print by artist Utagawa Hiroshige, two men cross paths in the rain near Edo Bay in Kanazawa, a coastal area south of modern-day Yokohama. The figure at right wears a straw raincoat much like the one shown opposite. At first glance, he is a walking version of the bundles of straw in the fields nearby.

Travel during the Tokugawa Period

Today bullet trains whisk passengers along the Tōkaidō, the great highway linking Edo and Kyoto, in 137 minutes. In the Tokugawa period the 319 miles (513 kilometers) took two weeks to travel on foot.

The highways of Japan pulsated with processions of daimyo to and from Edo. The shoguns forced the lords of Japan to spend every other year in palaces that clustered around their castle. A daimyo had to travel in style, with an escort of samurai and porters commensurate to his rank. The wealthiest and proudest among them marched with several thousand men, who walked with a distinctive swagger and twirled poles to impress the commoners kneeling by the roadside. The scroll below depicts the parade of a middling daimyo. Many daimyo spent half their fiscal revenues on the costs of "alternate attendance," as this system was called, leaving little to build up a war chest.

To accommodate the increasing number of travelers, small settlements along the way grew into large post towns. A network of well-provisioned roads came to link the distant corners of Japan. This infrastructure fostered a tourism revolution. Ordinary travelers ventured forth and sought out local specialties and famous sights across the land.

31 A daimyo procession
(Undated)

Although travelers encountered breathtaking scenery along the Tōkaidō, the journey could also be cold, wet, and exhausting. Raincoats would have been worn even by samurai escorting a great lord on his annual processions between Edo and his castle.

Under the Great Peace, Japan imported almost no raw materials or food, the principal exceptions being animal and marine products from the northern isles and medicines from China and elsewhere. Useful things were often fashioned from inexpensive, renewable materials, such as the hemp palm (*shuro*) fibers used in this raincoat, or the rice straw used for the accompanying pair of sandals.

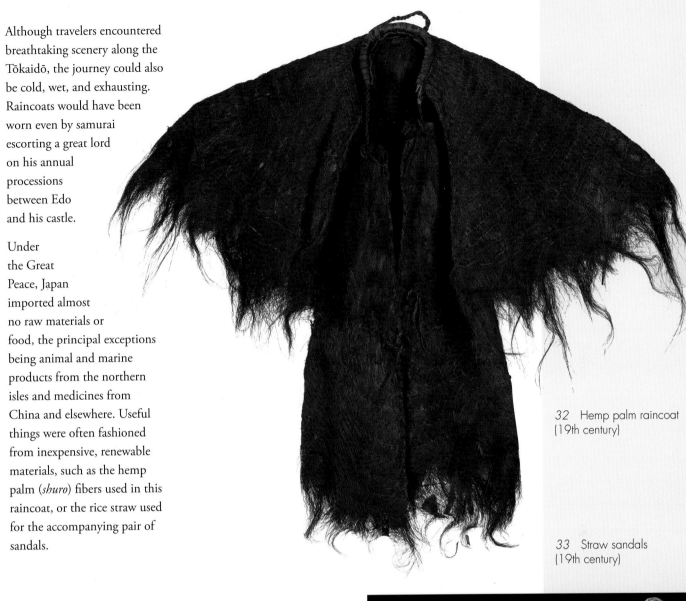

32 Hemp palm raincoat (19th century)

33 Straw sandals (19th century)

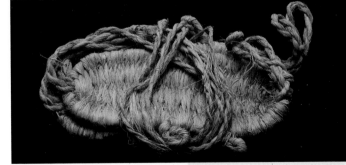

5

Armament or Ornament?

Armor was very rarely worn during the Great Peace. The main practical purpose of these assemblages of metal and silk, leather and lacquer was to serve as impressive decoration—not unlike a very expensive Christmas tree. Especially on New Year's, many samurai families would install one of their suits of armor in an alcove reserved for displays of art.

Why then is armor so prominent in "samurai" exhibitions throughout the world? The reason is that daimyo collections and the Japanese museums that curate them today have shaped the way that such exhibitions are organized even beyond Japan's shores. Daimyo collections divided their treasures into two categories, official and private objects (*omote-dōgu* and *oku-dōgu*). The latter are the lacquerware, ceramics, and precious textiles you will see in the following chapters. Swords, armor, and horse trappings made up the other category, "official objects." As with swords, a display of armor showcases the wealth and lineage of a warrior house. As with swords, the daimyo's political deployment of this art form has been remarkably successful at spreading a carefully crafted image of who the samurai were.

We invite you here to enjoy the technical accomplishments of Japan's armorers, but also to think about why these objects were made and preserved in the first place.

Opposite:
34   Detail of the ornamental gilt rim (*tehen kanamono*) on the crown of a samurai helmet bowl. This rim is decorated around the central opening (*tehen*) with a knob including the Date family mon. (17th to 19th century)

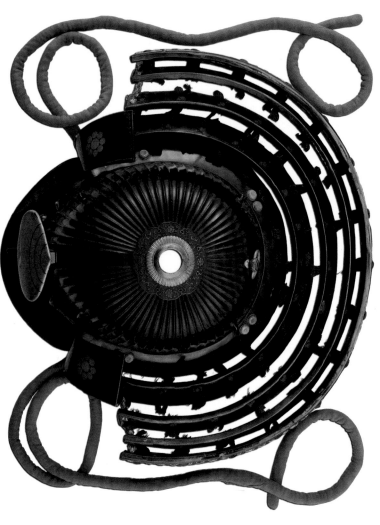

35, 36, 37 Samurai sleeves, helmet, and face guard (17th to 19th century)

The armor featured on this page comes from the collection of the Date ("Dah-tay") lords of Sendai, rulers of half a million subjects and among the greatest daimyo of Japan. The lands they owned produced more than 20 times as much rice as those of Lord Nishio (whose armor is on the opposite page). So grand were the Date that in 1613 they even sent a mission of three Japanese-built caravels to Mexico, and then to Madrid and Rome, where this samurai embassy created a sensation.

Unlike swords, armor was worn very rarely in the Tokugawa period. A daimyo's son might suit up for his coming-of-age ceremony, or a lord might don it during a procession. But mostly, it stayed packed in boxes, sorted into neatly labeled cloth bags. When armor was displayed, it usually sat on its box.

The suit of armor to the right was made for Lord Nishio, daimyo of Yokosuka. The Nishio, whose crest was a stylized pine tree with many trunks, were among the smaller daimyo houses of Japan, with an annual income of about 5,000 tons of rice.

The pouch on the lower left side of the chest plate was intended to store paper handkerchiefs and to prevent the swords that would have been pressed against the left side of the armor from scratching and chipping the lacquer.

Why the nipple rings?

A commander could tie his baton (*saihai*) or signaling fan to these hooks.

39 Samurai helmet and armor
(17th to 19th century)

38 Samurai helmet and armor
(18th century)

With its less intricate design, this armor was arguably the cheapest to produce of those shown here and was likely owned by a mid-ranking samurai. The helmet, too, is relatively plain. Its bowl is of a style used in the 16th century and could date to that era.

40 Samurai helmet
and armor
(17th to 19th century)

Many samurai helmets are utilitarian affairs, riveted together to protect the wearer in battle.

Others (known as *kawarikabuto*) were designed to be easily distinguished from a distance—to make it possible to spot a commander in the dust and confusion of battle, to allow a general to know who among his men performed particular feats of bravery, and to look impressive in ceremonies.

No other helmet is known to have golden sea urchins, carapaced and prickly. But a menagerie of other beasts bestrides Japanese helmets of this kind, from praying mantises to roaring dragons. In hand-to-hand battle, such extravagance could be lethal. Displayed in an alcove, it could be at once pleasingly whimsical and impressively ferocious.

Although the helmet bowl resembles a pre-16th-century style, the neck guard and sea urchins were added during the Tokugawa period.

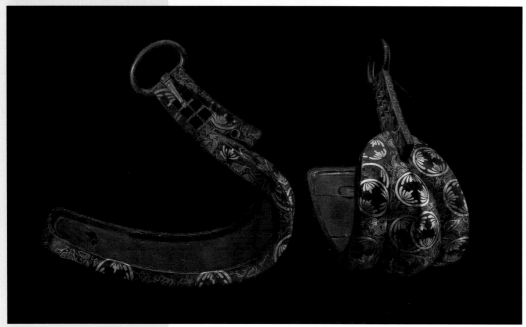

41 Stirrups
(18th century)
Signed, Kunitsugu,
resident of Kaga province

Japanese stirrups allow the rider to stand up on a relatively broad platform when shooting his bow. The open sides are a safety feature—unlike with Western stirrups, there is no danger of a horse dragging a fallen rider by his foot.

Everyday Wear

This is what samurai actually wore during the Great Peace. This magistrate (seated) poses in his *kamishimo*, the standard formal outfit for samurai of rank, consisting of a formal kimono, a split skirt, and a sleeveless vest with exaggerated shoulders. Note the two swords he wears in his sash, signs of his status as a samurai.

During the Great Peace, adult samurai and many other men shaved their pates and gathered the hair from the back of their head into a topknot. One popular theory claims that this kept the head cool under a helmet. But for an age when helmets were rarely worn, it seems more likely that the shaved pate reflected an intuitive understanding of why men's hairlines recede: to signal social maturity!

Wilhelm Heine was the staff artist of the Perry Expedition (1853–1854) dispatched by President Millard Fillmore to open Japan to American trade. The Americans went ashore in Hakodate to survey its harbor, which shortly thereafter became one of Japan's open ports.

Perhaps the magistrate was unhappy about this turn of events. But in paintings and early photographs, we rarely see a samurai crack a smile.

42
The magistrate of Hakodate with two attendants, sketched in 1854 by Wilhelm Heine.

6

Samurai Aesthetics: Extravagance and Restraint

Samurai, and especially the daimyo, showed off their wealth and status by displaying storied blades and splendid armor, golden screens, and intricate lacquerware. But unlike elites in most other parts of the early modern world, they often balanced this love of ostentation with a starker aesthetic of simplicity.

Two of the most important expressions of that aesthetic were the noh theater and the tea ceremony. Reflecting the influence of Zen practice, these cultural forms emphasize spare or imperfect materials, a reduction to essentials, simplicity of action, and a meditative atmosphere.

Opposite:
43 Box for writing implements (*hiramaki-e* and *takamaki-e* with gold alloys and silver) (18th century)

44 Interior of a box for writing implements (*hiramaki-e* and *takamaki-e* with gold alloys and silver) (18th century)

Lacquerware

When a daimyo's daughter married, she took with her a dowry of containers, writing boxes, cosmetic sets, and portable furniture, all covered in lacquer and precious metals. Many of these artifacts saw very little actual use. Rather, like swords and armor, they served as expressions of a family's wealth and rank, and were often kept in storage as heirlooms.

It is uncertain whether any of the objects in this section were part of a daimyo dowry, but several are of the highest quality and so well preserved as to suggest that they were handled infrequently and with great care.

But what is lacquer?

Lacquer is a finish derived from the sap of the tree *Toxicodendron vernicifluum*, which contains the same skin-irritating oil as poison ivy. Applied in layers on a wooden substrate in conditions of high humidity, the refined sap cures into a hard substance impervious to water. In the hands of Japanese artisans, it became a material of lustrous beauty. Iron oxide, charcoal, or both, were used to color black lacquer, and cinnabar for red lacquer.

Already by the 16th century, Japanese lacquerware was prized throughout the world. In English, the term "japan" meant lacquer in the same way that we still call porcelain "china." In the 17th century, Europeans tried to learn the secrets of making lacquer, copying both the substance and the style of the Japanese artifacts. Over time their efforts became more successful, to the point that by 1905 a Japanese report complained that the lacquerware sold in New York's Japanese curio shops was actually made in Germany!

Sown Images (Maki-e)

In decorating their lacquer objects, Japanese artisans developed methods of "sprinkling" gold and silver into the design, known as *maki-e* (meaning literally "sown images"). Within *maki-e,* there are several different techniques.

The most labor-intensive is known as *togidashi maki-e*, meaning "polished *maki-e*": the metallic design is covered with many layers of black lacquer that are then polished away with charcoal and water until the design reappears as part of a smooth, flat surface.

Hiramaki-e, or "flat *maki-e*," features a nearly flat design with a protective layer of transparent lacquer over the metal. The use of very small particles of metal and a dyed yellow lacquer results in a reddish tone.

In *takamaki-e*, or "raised *maki-e*," three-dimensional effects are achieved by "sprinkling" on top of patterns built up using lacquer and charcoal.

45 Lacquer tray with animal figures and eclipse (*takamaki-e*) (Early 18th century)

This exquisite tray contained a mystery: Why is the circle in the sky black? X-ray fluorescence analysis has revealed that the artist intentionally brushed black lacquer onto a golden sun. What we see is therefore an annular eclipse. Such eclipses were visible over Japan just six times in the Tokugawa period.

From the tree, a monkey with a face of carved coral peers down on a second figure by the lakeshore. Is he guarding the shrine at this ominous moment?

46 *The Popular Type*
Hayarisō
From the series
32 Modern-Day Types
Tōsei sanjūni sō
(ca. 1822–1823)

Lacquer items were not just for ostentatious display, but also for everyday use. In this print by Utagawa Kunisada, a young woman, who has just finished tying her hair up into the fashionable style of the day, applies makeup to her eyebrows with the help of a black lacquer mirror.

48 Small box
(*togidashi* and *takamaki-e* with gold and silver pattern)
(16th century)

This remarkable container was probably a comb box. All 20 inside and outside surfaces are decorated with heavy gold. The surfaces with the landscape are *takamaki-e*, while all remaining surfaces are *togidashi*. The four sides of the box depict a continuous landscape, as shown below. The exposed edges of the top and bottom are metallic silver to protect them from wear.

47 Bronze mirror
with lacquer container
(*hiramaki-e*)
(Late 18th century)

The decorations on this mirror—a pine tree, bamboo, cranes, and a tortoise—are all longevity symbols. Perhaps they cheered up its owner as, over time, more and more wrinkles appeared on his or her reflected face!

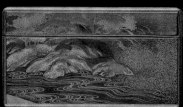

The *Kamakura-bori* technique uses a carved wood substrate overlaid with many layers of red and black lacquer. The design of cranes and hanging wisteria on this box is Japanese, whereas the borders and background are characteristic of Chinese cinnabar lacquerware from the Ming dynasty. The magnificent use of red and rubbed black lacquer is evidence of a master artisan.

49 Stationery box (*Kamakura-bori* style) (18th century)

50 Presentation box featuring spiny lobsters (*takamaki-e* with gold and cinnabar) (Mid-19th century)

51 Vanity box with articles
and mirror (*hiramaki-e*)
(19th century)

52 Black lacquer inrō depicting a kite tethered to a tree (five compartments) With ivory netsuke and silver ojime (17th century)

53 Gold inrō with wooden netsuke of a monk, and carnelian ojime (18th century)

Inrō

The word *inrō* refers to small containers carried at the waist by samurai and townsmen in the Tokugawa period. These were functional objects, typically used to hold seals or medicine, but they were also one of the principal male fashion accessories at the time.

We might think of the inrō as not unlike the necktie. Like modern-day office workers, samurai had fairly limited fashion choices, and the inrō allowed a bit of personal style and flair. Wealthy merchants had more flexibility in their dress, but they too used ornately decorated inrō as a conspicuous display of status.

Inrō are usually made up of three to five stacked compartments, held together by a cord and fastener, known as an *ojime*, and hung from the sash around the waist. The cord is secured to the sash by a toggle known as a *netsuke*. Netsuke were also personalized, miniature ornaments and—with their often whimsically humorous designs—remain a favorite of collectors today.

The Tea Ceremony

The Japanese tea ceremony takes the simple act of drinking tea and transforms it into an experience removed from the everyday.

Central to the experience are the aesthetic ideals of *wabi* and *sabi*, terms with a range of meanings at whose heart lies the appreciation of simplicity and imperfection. A typical tearoom, which might have been quite expensive, appears remarkably spare: plain tatami flooring and an alcove for the display of a single art object, such as a scroll or flower arrangement. And the implements themselves, although they can be quite beautiful, are meant to calm the mind with their simplicity and encourage spiritual self-cultivation with their imperfections, asymmetry, and signs of wear.

Samurai embraced the tea ceremony as a space in which people of different rank could share an intimate moment of contemplation.

The tea ceremony was also a space to demonstrate superior taste by declaring, for example, that an object unremarkable to the untrained eye was in fact priceless. In the 16th century, European visitors marveled that warlords would pay more than 10,000 gold coins for a simple earthenware tea caddy, which in Europe "would have no other use than to put it in a bird's cage as a drinking-trough."

54 Hanging scroll
(1717)

Artist Tsurusawa Tanzan (1655–1729), an accomplished student of Kanō Tan'yū (1602–1674), founded the Tsurusawa line of the Kanō school and was appointed official painter at the imperial court in Kyoto around the turn of the 17th century. This painting depicts a dragon in the conventional Chinese style as it emerges from spiraling whirlwinds.

Such a scroll would appear in the decorative alcove of a tearoom, signaling the season, the theme of the gathering, or a particular interest of one of the guests.

55 Flower vase
Possibly Takatori kiln
(19th to 20th century)

56 Tea caddy and bag
(18th to 19th century)

This stoneware tea caddy features an ivory lid and is accompanied by a fitted brocade bag for storage.

57 Stoneware water jar
with black lacquer lid
(19th to 20th century)

The box-like shape of this water container, created by artisan Asami Gorōsuke, is known as *eboshi*, after the hats worn by court nobles. The bluish tinge is created through the use of rice straw in the glaze.

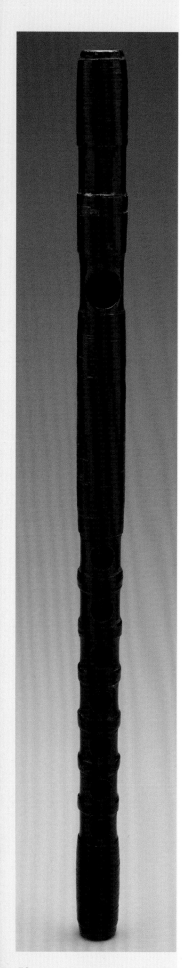

58   *Ryūteki* flute
(Late 19th century)

The *ryūteki* is a transverse, or side-blown, flute used in traditional Japanese court music. The flute used in noh, known as the *nōkan*, developed out of the *ryūteki* and is nearly identical in size and appearance.

As recounted in a moving episode in the medieval epic *The Tale of the Heike*, a famous *ryūteki* known as Greenleaf (J. Aoba) was carried into battle by the young Heike noble Atsumori. When Kumagae, a rough warrior from the rival Minamoto clan, found the flute on the boy's body after taking his life in battle, he recalled having heard the flute being played in the enemy camp the night before. Moved to tears, he renounced the world and became a monk. This episode was later adapted for the noh theater as the play *Atsumori*.

Noh Theater

The darkness enshrouding noh and the beauty that arises from this constitute a unique world of shadows which we find today only on the stage.

—Tanizaki Jun'ichirō,
In Praise of Shadows (1933)

Noh is a form of theater whose origins lie in ancient commoner performance, but which in the medieval period became one of the preferred entertainments of the warrior elite, a status it maintained under the Great Peace. Noh plays are texts of great beauty and poetry, and performances are remarkable for their relative simplicity.

A typical Tokugawa-period performance would have taken place not in a theater, but on a covered outdoor stage, often at dusk. As darkness descended, the ethereal qualities of noh emerged to their fullest: the haunting yelps of the drummers, the wail of the flute, the rhythmic chanting of the chorus, and the glimmer of brocade by torchlight.

Noh masks are among the most immediately recognizable symbols of the Japanese theater. Objects of intricate craftsmanship, they are treated with reverence by the actors who use them to transform into their roles. The masks often seem to change appearance depending on the angle at which they are viewed, and by raising or lowering his face an actor can convey subtle differences of emotion.

The *shōjō*, a water sprite from Chinese mythology with an apelike body and human face, gives its name to a celebratory noh play in which one features as the principal character. The shōjō mask is that of an adolescent male, but with a gentle smile reflecting the creature's amiable personality. Strands of hair seem to be plastered to the forehead, as if it had just emerged from the water. Most striking of all is the red pigmentation, suggesting the shōjō's remarkable fondness for drink and perpetual state of mild intoxication.

The mask at right is inscribed on the inside with the name Shunwaka, a 15th-century artisan who ranks among the most famous of all noh mask carvers. However, the mask was made a full two centuries after Shunwaka's era, and the inscription was likely added sometime after its creation.

Opposite:
59   *Shōjō* mask
(Likely 17th century)

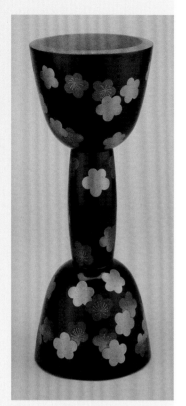

The noh musical ensemble consists of a chorus of chanters accompanied by three drummers and a flutist. Each drummer plays a different variety of drum: in descending order of size, the upright drum (*shime-daiko*), hip drum (*ōtsuzumi*), and shoulder drum (*kotsuzumi*). The thwacks of the drums combine with piercing yelps, rhythmic chanting, and the plaintive wails of the flute to create the unique aural atmosphere of noh. These sounds also provide important rhythmic cues to the actors.

The drum on the right is a hip drum. The two drum heads are held in place by a black lacquer core and several meters of red fiber rope. At left is the core from a smaller shoulder drum, featuring black lacquer and a decorative flower pattern.

61 Hip drum
(Likely early 18th century)

60 Shoulder drum core
(Early 19th century)

Noh robes are celebrated for their sumptuous materials and elaborate, colorful designs. Traditionally they were given as gifts by wealthy patrons to their favorite troupes or actors.

The robes tend to be quite large, and the fabric is stiff and heavy. The effect on stage is to create a striking theatricality, as the individuality of the actor's body is flattened into a singular field of glinting, intricate patterns.

62   Noh robe
(Late 18th century)

This type of robe (at right,
front view; below, open
back view), known as an
atsuita, is used for male
roles, as well as gods and
demons. Like the *karaori*
(opposite), its name derives from
the fabric from which it is made. *Atsuita* feature
dynamic, eye-catching geometrical designs,
although in performance they are often partly
obscured beneath broad-sleeved outer robes. The
robe here, with a bold thunderbolt pattern that
zigzags across the fabric, is for a warrior role.

Opposite:
63   Noh robe
(Likely 18th century)

This robe (at left, front view;
at right, open back view), for
a female role, is composed of
a patchwork of three distinct
patterns recycled from what were
originally separate garments.
The combination creates a
striking visual effect, as does the
metallic thread, which would
have glinted mysteriously in the
flickering torchlight of a traditional
performance.

The robe is an example of the
type known as *karaori*, used
primarily for female roles. The
word, meaning literally "Chinese
weave," refers also to the thick,
stiff fabric from which such robes
are made, and points to the fact
that such textiles were originally
imported from the continent.

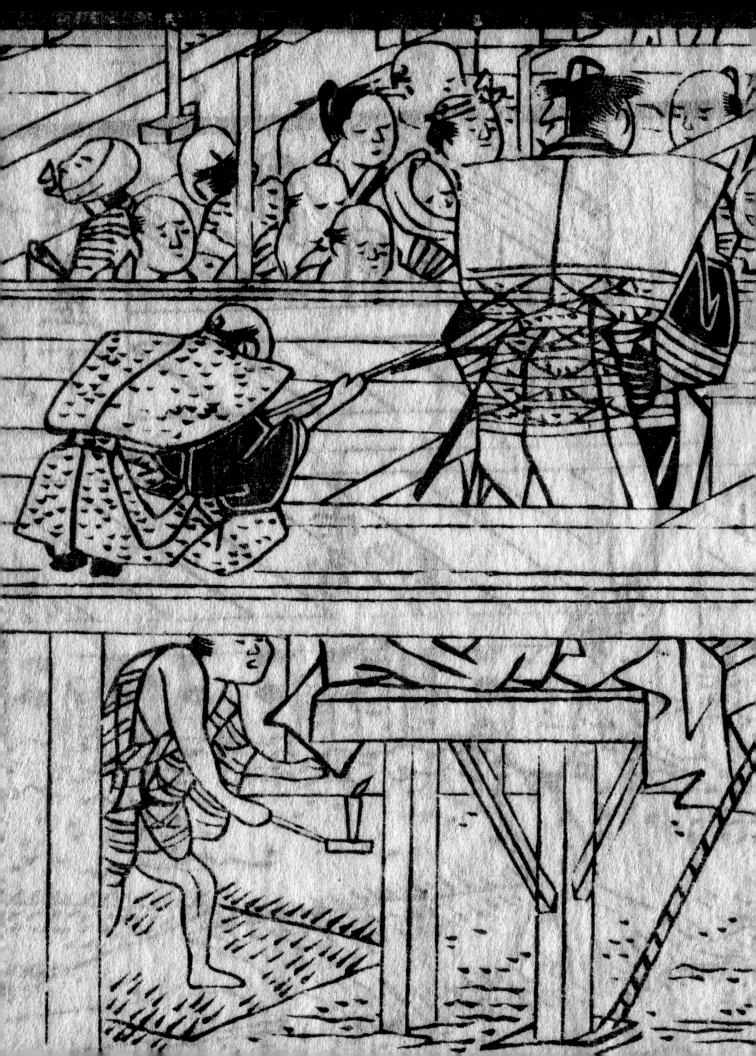

7

The Samurai Imagined

While the samurai presided over the Tokugawa order, urban commoners created a popular culture that was diverse, prolific, and ever-changing. With a few coppers in his coin purse, a visitor to Edo, Kyoto, or Osaka would have had his choice of entertainments.

Popular fiction and vibrant color prints beckoned from bookstore shelves. A variety of street performers vied for the attention of passersby: animal trainers, soapbox orators, musclemen, illusionists, "freaks," and more. In the theater districts, the lavish spectacle of kabuki and the puppet theater brought to life tales of men and women torn between passion and duty.

Not surprisingly, the samurai loomed large in this popular culture. During the Great Peace, most real-life samurai died on their futons after long years of guard duty or bookkeeping, with few opportunities for flamboyant displays of martial valor or loyalty to their lords. But in ballads, plays, fictional narratives, and woodblock prints, they were men of mettle and action, swinging their swords and laying down their lives in the service of higher ideals.

This reimagining of the samurai still reverberates in the present.

Opposite:
64   Detail from
*Illustrated Encyclopedia
of the Theater
Shibai kinmōzui*
(1803, Meiji-era printing)

65 *Chūshingura, Act XI: The Night Raid*
Chūshingura jūichidanme yo-uchi no zu
(ca. 1831)

Utagawa Kuniyoshi's fanciful rendering of the climactic night raid features a stark, moonlit streetscape with Western-style buildings. Western illustrations offered a new source of inspiration for Japanese artists in the Edo period. Kuniyoshi took the general conception for this print from an illustration in a 17th-century book on the Dutch West and East Indies by the adventurer Joan (or Johan) Nieuhof. The original depicts residences in Batavia (modern-day Jakarta), the capital of the Dutch East Indies.

The 47 Ronin

In a realm at peace, the loyalty and bravery of worthy samurai remain hidden. But they are as stars which, unseen by day, emerge at night in all their brightness.

> —*Chūshingura*, or *A Treasury of Loyal Retainers* (1748)

It all began with a moment of rashness in the spring of 1701. Inside the halls of Edo Castle, the daimyo Asano Naganori, apparently under provocation, drew his sword and attacked the senior shogunal official Kira Yoshinaka. For this grave offense, he was ordered to commit suicide, and his retainers became ronin, or masterless samurai. Two years later, 47 of these retainers emerged from the shadows and avenged Asano's death in spectacular fashion, scaling the walls of Kira's estate by cover of darkness and taking their enemy's head.

No tale of samurai valor so captivated the Tokugawa masses. Unlike the warriors of ages past who dominated in fiction and on stage, the 47 ronin were heroes of the present era. Their actions showed that the samurai ideals of loyalty, honor, and martial readiness had not completely disappeared in a realm at peace.

Two months after completing their vendetta, the surviving ronin were themselves ordered to commit suicide. Within days an Edo theater mounted the first dramatization of their story. Many more theatrical versions followed. The most famous of these, titled *Chūshingura*, or *A Treasury of Loyal Retainers*, had its premiere in 1748.

Chūshingura paints a sweeping picture of the retainer's trials and travails as they plot their revenge. The play also established what would become the conventional historical disguise and surrogate names for the characters. Because contemporary events were officially off-limits under the Tokugawa regime, the action was set in the distant past—an established work-around which was completely transparent to theatergoers. *Chūshingura* was so popular that the very name soon became a stand-in for the actual historical incident. Such is the case with Shungyōsai's version, which strives for detail and faithfulness to actual events, but which, to be published at all, had to adopt the conventional historical disguise.

An Illustrated Chūshingura
Ehon Chūshingura
(1800)

66a   One of the most popular acts in the play depicts the exploits of the chief retainer, Yuranosuke. To throw his enemies off the scent, Yuranosuke pretends to be an irredeemable playboy with no possible intention of carrying out a vendetta. Here he is seen reveling in the Gion pleasure quarters in Kyoto with his favorite courtesan, Kashiwagi, along with a party of male and female entertainers.

Characteristically, the account in this more "authentic" version, written and illustrated by Hayami Shungyōsai, departs from the theatrical version in several ways. Kashiwagi is later revealed to be a merchant's daughter named Okaru. Although the theatrical version includes an extended love affair between Okaru and Kanpei, another retainer, this subplot is completely absent in Shungyōsai's telling, which instead pairs Okaru (Kashiwagi) and Yuranosuke.

66b   A drunken Yuranosuke playfully takes a brush in hand and prepares to write on the ceiling. At his side, a young woman holds an inkstone aloft, while Kashiwagi (center) and the others look on in amusement.

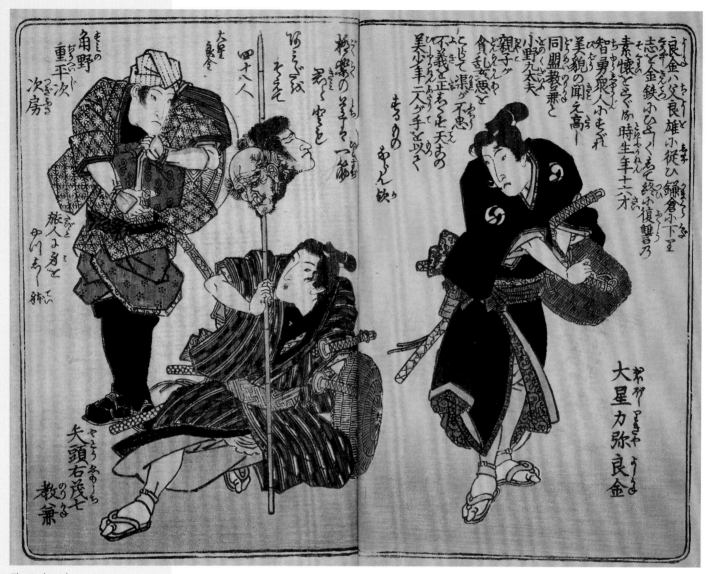

The Iroha Library
Iroha bunko
(1836–1872)

67a In the print above, on the right-hand page, Yuranosuke's son, Ōboshi Rikiya, is praised in the accompanying text as brave, iron-willed, and "famously handsome." At left is Sumino [Sugino] Jūheiji, disguised as a traveler, and Yatō Emoshichi, grasping a pike bearing the heads of Ono Kudayū, traitor to the cause and spy for the villain Kō no Moronao (the stand-in for Kira Yoshinaka in the conventional historical disguise), and his son, the bandit Sadakurō.

The sprawling work *The Iroha Library*—the title of which derives from the coincidence that the Japanese syllabary, or *iroha*, contains 47 characters—was published serially over the course of more than three and a half decades. Like *An Illustrated Chūshingura*, it is in part an attempt at a historically accurate account of the vendetta: "the true, authentic story" (*seishi jitsuden*), as Shunsui's own subtitle puts it. Nevertheless, the conventional historical disguise remains, and the story is freely embellished and peppered with the anachronistic vernacular of the late Tokugawa period.

The Iroha Library was one of the first works of Japanese literature to appear in English translation. The English version, translated by Shiuichiro Saito and Edward Greey under the title *The Loyal Ronins*, was published in 1880, the same year as the first English translation of *Chūshingura* itself. Although the choice might now seem somewhat odd, Saito selected this particular work as a representative example of contemporary popular Japanese literature, and for its insights into "Japanese life under the feudal system."

Among the translation's enthusiastic readers was none other than Theodore Roosevelt, whose admiration for *bushidō* ("the way of the samurai") is said to have inclined him to sympathize with the Japanese when he mediated at the negotiations to conclude the Russo-Japanese War in 1905.

67b The main image depicts the swordsmith Ōmi of Settsu province (right) and his disciple Tsuda Sukehiro as they forge a sword for Yuranosuke's right-hand man Onodera Jūnai, shown in the inset at upper left. Sukehiro's actions illustrate that the virtue of loyalty extended even to the lowest-ranking retainers. Sukehiro was originally Jūnai's servant, but after hearing his master mocked for the poor condition of his sword, he apprenticed with Ōmi to make him a proper one. Jūnai carried this sword with him on the night of the raid.

67c To the right, we see the same episode depicted in the second scene from *An Illustrated Chūshingura* (shown on page 57). A drunken Yuranosuke writes on the ceiling as two of his companions look on with glee.

68   *A View of the Flourishing of Kabuki in Edo*
Odori keiyō Edo-e no sakae
(1858)

Theater

Within months of its premiere at an Osaka puppet theater, *Chūshingura* had been adapted for live actors on the kabuki stage.

Kabuki was the most popular form of theater in the Tokugawa period. In 1603, the same year the Tokugawa shogunate was founded in Edo, women appeared in the public spaces of Kyoto and began to attract crowds with routines that combined music, dance, and pantomime. These performances soon acquired the name *kabuki*, a word originally connoting their offbeat, eccentric qualities.

By the mid-18th century, kabuki had developed into a baroque spectacle staged for boisterous crowds in large, technologically sophisticated theaters. It had also come to be performed exclusively by men. After a series of public disturbances resulting from the erotically charged atmosphere of early kabuki, women were banned from the stage in 1629 and boys in 1652.

At left, artist Utagawa Kunisada's depiction of the interior of a kabuki theater shows the dramatic entrance of the superhuman warrior Kamakura Gongorō in the play *Just a Minute!* (*Shibaraku*, premiered 1697). A group of nobles faces imminent execution at the hands of their villainous captors. At just the right moment, Gongorō cries out from offstage the famous line that gives the play its title. Seconds later he storms out onto the *hanamichi*—kabuki's distinctive walkway linking the back of the theater to the stage—allowing the audience a close-up look.

This particular play is a traditional showpiece for the Ichikawa Danjūrō line of actors. On the basis of the year the print was produced, the actor here is presumably Kawarasaki Gonjūrō I (1838–1903), who became Danjūrō IX in 1874. Nevertheless, this is most likely an imagined performance: the crests above the stage belong to all three of Edo's rival licensed theaters.

69   *The Prosperity of the Eastern Capital*
Tōto han'ei no zu
(1854)

The scene below is from a set of three triptychs of the three licensed theaters in Edo's Saruwaka-chō theater district at the close of the Tokugawa period. This is the street scene outside the Nakamura Theater. The drum tower, a symbol of official license, features the theater's crest, while the painted signboards beneath advertise scenes from the current plays as well as the names of the actors.

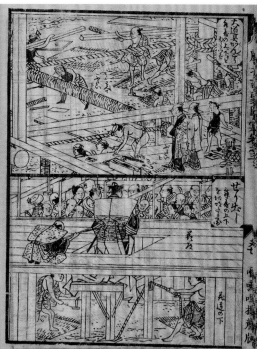

70a Sophisticated stage technology was key to many of the spectacular effects seen in kabuki. The top of this illustration shows a backdrop that can be rotated along a horizontal axis for a sudden scene change. At bottom right, we see a samurai rising into view on the small stage elevator known as the *suppon*, used for dramatic entrances on the *hanamichi* walkway.

70b Among the many pages devoted to props and costumes is the following set of four images. At upper right, we see the evil magician Nikki Danjō disguised as a rat in the play *The Fragrant Bush Clover of Sendai* (*Meiboku sendai hagi*, premiered 1777). Continuing counterclockwise, we see actors playing a frog, a fox, and a wild boar.

Illustrated Encyclopedia of the Theater
Shibai kinmozui
(1803, Meiji-era printing)

Written by Shikitei Sanba, one of the most popular authors of the early 19th century, *Illustrated Encyclopedia of the Theater* offers a comprehensive treatment of the world of kabuki. Readers are presented with detailed illustrations and textual accounts of nearly all aspects of the theater, including its history and conventions; set, costume, and theater design; and the cultures of theatergoing, connoisseurship, and fandom. The illustrations were created by Katsukawa Shun'ei and Utagawa Toyokuni I.

Music is indispensable to kabuki. Whereas the earliest ensembles were borrowed from noh, kabuki steadily incorporated new and diverse influences. One of the earliest and most important additions was the *shamisen*.

The *shamisen* is a three-stringed musical instrument not unlike a banjo in size, shape, and sound. The strings are plucked with a plectrum, yielding a distinctive twangy tone. The instrument arrived by way of the Ryukyu Islands (Okinawa) in the 16th century, and a similar three-stringed banjo known as the *sanshin* remains popular there today.

The *shamisen* provides the instrumental accompaniment to the narrative chanting used in the puppet theater. Accordingly, the many kabuki plays originally written for the puppet theater—of which *Chūshingura* is a famous example—feature the instrument prominently.

*71 Shamisen
(19th century)*

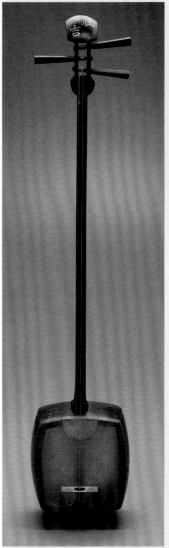

The title of the below collection of actor portraits, *Thirty-Six Flowers of the Stage*, puns on the term *sanjūrokkasen*, referring to the 36 "immortals" of classical Japanese verse. Here, however, the character for "flower" is used in place of the homophonous character for "poem," alluding to kabuki actors' status as one of the "flowers of Edo." Following a frontispiece depicting three major actors of the day are 12 illustrations of celebrated actors in character (two additional volumes were likely planned, but were never completed). All of the images are accompanied by poetry, much of it by the actors themselves.

*72 Thirty-Six Flowers
of the Stage
Yakusha Sanjūrokkasen
(1835)*

The portrait on the right-hand page is of Kataoka Ichizō I as the celebrated spearsman Gotō Mototsugu (1560–1615) in a historical drama from the early 1830s. On the left is Ichikawa Sumizō III as Oniō Shinzaemon in an 1833 play about the Soga brothers, whose 12th-century vendetta against their father's murderer was conventionally staged in one form or another at New Year's.

73 Woodblock for a fan print of *The Five Men: Kaminari ("Thunder") Shōkurō* Gonin otoko no uchi: *Kaminari Shōkurō* (ca. 1850)

Print Culture

The Tokugawa period was a golden age of print culture, as shown by the wide assortment of printed books and artistic prints in this catalog.

With rising incomes and literacy rates under the Great Peace, commercial publishing houses began to sprout up in the major cities. Already by the 1660s, all manner of texts once available only as hand-copied manuscripts were being sold in printed editions: Chinese and Japanese classics, medical treatises, dictionaries, popular fiction, poetry collections, and more.

As commercial concerns came to exert greater influence on literary production, new genres were born catering to the tastes of urban commoners. For the first time there arose what might be termed "professional" authors. There was also growing demand for illustrators. The earliest artistic prints were black-and-white illustrations for popular books, but by the end of the 17th century a flourishing market had emerged for single-sheet prints. Popular subjects included actors, courtesans, and landscapes.

The size and shape of artist Utagawa Kunisada's design suggest that the woodblock shown on the opposite page was used to produce a decorative print for a paper fan. Although no print survives from this particular block (fan prints are rare because they were functional objects), this creative reconstruction shows what the finished product might have looked like. Kunisada completed other prints of Shōkurō, and this recreation borrows aspects of these prints' color scheme and shading, as well as the use of Shōkurō's characteristic crest: two mallets and a drumhead, evoking the sound of thunder. The text in the cartouche at lower left reads "designed by Toyokuni upon request"—this request likely came from the publisher Sanoya Kihei, whose seal is immediately to the right.

The historical Shōkurō was a member of a gang of five outlaws who wreaked havoc in the city of Osaka until their arrest in the summer of 1701. Like the 47 samurai who famously became ronin that same year, the "five men"—by all accounts unredeemed villains in real life—were mythologized in popular accounts and in the theater. Reimagined as chivalrous outlaws defending the downtrodden and beholden to their own code of honor, they became commoner counterparts to the loyal retainers.

Many actors performed the role of Shōkurō in the final decades of the Tokugawa period. In the absence of identifying crests or a precise date, it is difficult to identify with certainty the actor represented here. On the basis of facial features alone, however, the most likely candidate is Ichikawa Danjūrō VIII, who performed the role in several different plays in the mid-19th century.

74   The Five Men:
Kaminari ("Thunder") Shōkurō
Gonin otoko no uchi:
Kaminari Shōkurō
(ca. 1850)
Recreation of woodblock print

Almost all printed materials in the Tokugawa period were produced using woodblocks such as the one at left, the key block (used for the black outline) for a fan print of an actor in the role of Kaminari ("Thunder") Shōkurō, a notorious gangster active in the city of Osaka around 1700.

By 1600, woodblock technology already had a nearly thousand-year history in Japan, having been used in Buddhist temples for the printing of sutras and other religious texts. The dawn of the Great Peace saw several noteworthy experiments with movable type, but woodblocks remained the preferred method up to and even beyond the Meiji Restoration. Not only were carved blocks well suited to a written language comprising thousands of characters—often written in a flowing, cursive calligraphic style—but they also allowed the easy reproduction of combinations of text and image.

Although the technology grew increasingly sophisticated over the course of the Tokugawa period, the basic method remained the same. The final copy of the text, image, or both was written on thin, transparent paper, which was pasted upside-down onto blocks of wood. Specialist block-carvers then carved away the white spaces. The resulting blocks could be used to print hundreds of faithful copies of the original.

Chinese vernacular fiction was enormously popular in the late Tokugawa period. The conceit of *The Actors' Romance of the Three Kingdoms* is to replace the three kingdoms of *The Romance of the Three Kingdoms* with the three major cities of Japan and their rival theatrical scenes. The theaters' histories, and the competition among them, are recounted in mock-historical narratives, after which appears a succession of multicolored prints of famous actors of the day in their roles.

The Actors' Romance of the Three Kingdoms
Yakusha fūzoku sangokushi
(1831)

75a Here we see the climactic confrontation between the superhuman hero Arajishi Otokonosuke (right) and the evil magician Nikki Danjō (left) in the play *The Fragrant Bush Clover of Sendai* (we encountered Danjō earlier on page 62, disguised as a rat, in *Illustrated Encyclopedia of the Theater*). Although the actors and roles are not labeled, from the facial features, actors' crests, and date of publication, the illustration appears to be of an 1830 Kyoto production starring Matsumoto Kōshirō V as Danjō (Kōshirō is recognizable by his long, pointed nose and close-set eyes) alongside his son Ichikawa Komazō V (who later became Kōshirō VI).

75b Three actors are depicted in the guise of the "three brothers" from *The Romance of the Three Kingdoms*: Liu Bei, Guan Yu, and Zhang Fei.

75c Two theater enthusiasts are shown engaging in the popular amateur art of actor impersonation. The man on the right performs vocal mimicry while his friend provides musical accompaniment.

76   *A Humorous Collection of Jewels of the Floating World*
Dōke ukiyo tama-zukushi
(1864)

The "floating world" (*ukiyo*) in the title of this triptych by artist Utagawa Yoshitora refers to the heady pleasures of Edo urban life, including the theater, the brothel quarters, and all manner of street entertainment. The prints are an example of an "enumeration" or "exhaustive listing" (*tsukushi* or *zukushi*), an artistic and literary device wherein words with a common component are wittily presented in close succession. In this case, the common link is the word *tama*, whose range of meanings includes "jewel," "ball," "bubble," and "soul."

The tama (or *dama*) here are conjured by the illusionist at center. To point to but a few figures amidst the triptych's rich jumble, at bottom right we see a man as he releases a fart (*hedama*)—visualized as bubbles—to fend off a mischievous water sprite. Above him is a bubble-vendor (*tamaya*), whose umbrella doubles as a conspicuous advertisement. Such vendors sold wands and liquid soap, and attracted hordes of children in their wake.

In the upper left is the kabuki actor Ichikawa Danjūrō (popularly known as "the boss," or *oyadama*) in one of his most famous roles: as the superhuman warrior Kamakura Gongorō in the play *Just a Minute!* He is seen with his oversized sword, red pleated trousers emblazoned with the Danjūrō crest, and distinctive red and white face makeup.

善助夫婦
花見る連立て
老人を廁る図

8

Death and
the Good Life

During Japan's Great Peace, different visions contended about the meaning of death and how to live a good, responsible life. In exploring these, we hear echoes of our own needs and hopes—to reach out to the dead across the chasm of bereavement, to raise our children well and repay our parents' love, to avoid disease and danger, and to put off death as long as possible.

But Tokugawa worldviews can also differ starkly from our own. By engaging with them, we can arrive at new perspectives on our own world, realizing that some of what we regard as universally true is in fact the product of our own particular time, place, and culture.

Opposite:
77   Detail from
A Mirror of People's Hearts
Banmin kokoro no kagami
(1854)

Becoming an Ancestral Deity

Virtually all Tokugawa subjects were Buddhists, at least on paper. Before the Great Peace, Japanese Buddhism offered laypeople two possibilities for the afterlife: yet another turn in the cycle of rebirth and suffering, or rebirth into the "Pure Land" paradise of Amida, the Buddha of Infinite Light.

In the 1600s, Buddhist temples began to advertise another possibility: at a very reasonable price, they could help people transform their parents' souls into divine ancestral spirits. The offer must have been appealing. It allowed people to imagine that the dead were still with them, and to look forward to a serene future when they themselves would join the collectivity of the household's ancestors.

These beliefs reshaped the way people imagined their place in time and across the thresholds of birth and death. And they left a material legacy in the form of the ancestral tablets and small household shrines that formed the spiritual heart of each household.

78 The bodhisattva Kannon of eleven faces and a thousand hands (1692, inscribed)

Across Japan, small shrines (*zushi*) served as household altars where the living could remember the dead and the ancestral spirits themselves might dwell. One German visitor to Japan in the 1690s claimed that "every house [in Japan] had to own a *zushi*" to prove that they were Buddhists rather than adherents of the forbidden "evil faith" of Christianity.

Although it is hard to imagine that many poor families owned pieces of the quality displayed here, zushi shrines were produced in great numbers and many hundreds have found their way into collections across Europe and the United States.

Bodhisattvas are enlightened beings who defer nirvana to save other sentient beings from suffering. Kannon is short for Kanzeon Bosatsu, "the bodhisattva who hears the cries of the world." This statue of Kannon has many hands, each holding a different symbol of power, to allow her compassion to reach the entire world.

Like Buddhism itself, Kannon came to Japan from India by way of China. On the journey, the bodhisattva changed gender. In India his name was Avalokiteśvara, but in East Asia the deity assumed the qualities of a merciful mother.

Mortuary tablets (*ihai*) are memorials to dead family members, as well as dwelling places for their souls. They are inscribed not with the names the dead bore in life, but with posthumous ordination names (*kaimyō*) they received at their funerals. This custom emerged from deathbed ordinations when a dying layman sought to gain extra merit by drawing his last breaths as a monk. Under the Great Peace, virtually all dead Japanese received such names, as they do to this day.

79 Memorial tablet

This tablet takes the form of a tombstone emerging from a lotus flower base. The lotus grows in the mud but emerges unsullied, a property that has made it a Buddhist symbol of purity and hope. The tablet commemorates a man and a woman. He died in 1729, she in 1755.

80 Memorial tablet

This tablet commemorates two men and two women, who may have been a husband (d. 1729) and wife (d. 1754), along with their son (d. 1769) and daughter-in law (d. 1766). The dates are inscribed on the back.

81, 82 Folding screens
Scenes from *The 24 Paragons
of Filial Piety*
(Late 17th to early 19th century)

Filial Piety

In China, loving, lifelong obedience to parents—usually translated as "filial piety"—is a cardinal Confucian virtue. A 13th-century Chinese collection called *The 24 Paragons of Filial Piety* tells the stories of sons and daughters who exemplified this ideal:

Guo Ju dug his own son's grave, intent on taking the boy's life to save his aging mother from hunger. Lao Laizi, a mature scholar, dressed as a boy and played with his toys to give his elderly parents a taste of their long-lost youth. Lu Ji, only six years old, stole oranges to feed his mother. Lady Tang breastfed her toothless mother-in-law. Wu Meng let mosquitoes drink freely of his blood that his parents might sleep unmolested. Yu Qianlou tasted his father's stool to diagnose his affliction. And so on.

Like so many other aspects of Chinese thought, these stories crossed the sea and became part of Japan's cultural heritage. The stories of the 24 paragons were reproduced in many printed books and works of art. The artist of these screens took pains to depict the scenes in an ancient Chinese setting, with dress, hairstyles, and architecture distinct from those of Tokugawa Japan (or its contemporary, Qing China).

Responsible Parenthood

The people of Tokugawa Japan prided themselves on being filial children and honoring their ancestors. They also saw themselves as affectionate, responsible parents. Why then is it that on this page, we see illustrations of mothers crushing their babies?

Governments and social activists printed these books to convince people to raise all of their children. In this effort, they faced formidable challenges: in the 1700s, every other child was killed at birth in some regions of Japan. Their people did not think of a newborn child as a person. Rather, personhood was attained gradually through a series of milestones. They therefore did not speak of killing babies, but of "sending them back" to the spirit world to be born again at a more opportune time.

Parents believed it necessary to limit the number of children they had, so as to properly provide for those who mattered most in their lives. Infanticide allowed them to maintain the family line for their ancestors, to ensure a pleasant retirement for their parents, and to raise their chosen children with the care they deserved.

Moral suasion of the kind reprinted in these pages, along with childrearing subsidies and pregnancy surveillance, challenged the culture of infanticide in the course of the 19th century. It persisted locally into the 20th century, but by 1920 the infanticidal parts of Japan were transformed. By 1920, couples whose grandparents had grown up with one or two siblings now raised six or seven children.

83   A Guide to the Prosperity of Future Generations
Shison hanjō tebikigusa
(Undated edition, but similar in style to dated editions from between 1826 and 1857)

The illustration on the right-hand page shows a woman killing her newborn baby. The artist gave her a conventionally beautiful face and dressed her in nice clothes, implying that she is not poor. Infanticides in Japan always happened immediately after the birth of the child, but this artist has chosen to give the newborn the look of a much older infant that no Japanese parent would consider harming. Presumably he was trying to convey that newborn children, too, were human beings.

To the left, the woman is seen again, this time with horns, fangs, claws, bug-eyes, and animal ears. "This is what the heart of a person looks like who 'returns' children," the text explains. In other words: kill babies and you have lost your humanity.

84   Personal copybook with a handwritten copy of Manual for Ensuring the Prosperity of Future Generations
Shison hanjō tebikigusa
(ca. 1835, a date that appears in another part of the book)

The Guide to the Prosperity of Future Generations was first written in 1793 and reprinted in at least 20 different editions over the next 80 years. People seem to have taken its message to heart. Here, an amateur has copied the text and illustrations into a notebook, perhaps with the intention of lecturing his fellow villagers.

The writing around the illustrations, however, is not from the *Guide*, but consists of magic spells.

85   Avoid Evil and Do Good!
Japanese Verses on Extending Life and Rearing Children
Shoaku bakusaku, shozen bugyō enmei kosodate wasan
(Probably early to mid-19th century)

The opponents of infanticide were very savvy in spreading their message. This is a book of jingles warning against infanticide, designed to be easily learned and repeated. It closes with this illustration.

On the first page (right), a woman wears a sweatband on her brow, suggesting that she has just given birth. We see her suffocating her child, while her husband brings a bucket, presumably a make-shift coffin, and holds a hoe to dig a grave for the body.

Speech bubbles show us the futures of these three souls. The baby soars into the embrace of Kannon, the bodhisattva of mercy, who welcomes it with all eight arms. The father is dragged off by an ox-faced demon, while the mother hurtles to hell on a fiery chariot.

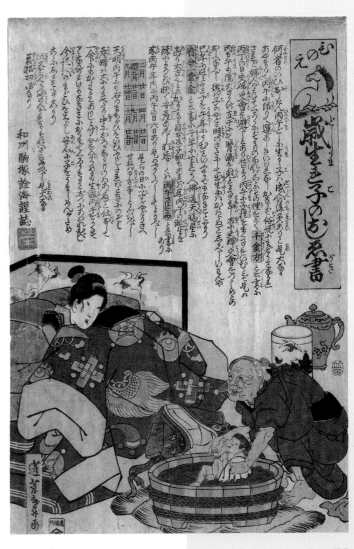

86   On Children Born in a Fire-Horse Year
Hinoeuma umareko no oshiegaki
(Undated, but known to be 1845)

This print shows a happy birth scene: the mother, still resting against a pile of futons, watches the midwife bathe her baby. Yet the purpose of the print is not to celebrate, but to save the lives of newborn girls.

In deciding which children to raise and which to "return" to the spirit world, parents could consult a wide variety of techniques to predict the child's future. According to the East Asian zodiac cycle, 1846 was a year of the fire-horse. Popular belief had it that girls born in that year would grow up to lead tragically destructive lives. This poster argues against this view.

It does so not, as we might expect, by challenging the basic assumption that days could be lucky or unlucky, but by citing Chinese authorities arguing for the auspiciousness of births in "horse" years. Perhaps that is why there is a horse in the title cartouche. The large block of yellow highlighting in the middle of the text lists the six fire-horse days in the fire-horse year of 1846, and reassures readers that all will be well so long as they do not make a baby on those days.

A Tale of Two Lives

The two volumes of *A Mirror of People's Hearts*, written by a medical doctor in 1854, are perhaps the most artistically interesting of over a hundred similar books urging readers to raise all their children.

It tells the stories of two families. The first volume follows the life of Zensuke ("good fellow"). A farm boy near Kyoto, he grows up poor, but through a lifetime of hard work, honesty, and generosity becomes a wealthy man and leaves his 12 (!) children in honor and affluence.

The second takes us to the mountains of the Northeast, a region then infamous for infanticide, and also the place where the book was written, carved, and printed. Itarō ("First-born Swine") and his brothers ("Pig 2" and "Pig 3") live a life of vice, indolence, and cruelty to small animals. When their wives become pregnant, they have abortions or kill the newborn babies. At the end of their lives, they have no one to care for them, and their souls ultimately go to hell.

The Good Life

87a   Zensuke (at lower left) makes straw sandals while his parents (at right) and his younger children eat. Note how many children he has! The eldest son (at left) is already old enough to help with the farm work. The eldest daughter makes herself useful by carrying one of the babies on her back. Zensuke's wife nurses one child while carrying another on her back.

87b   Zensuke carries his old father to a cherry blossom viewing spot, while his wife leads her mother-in-law by the hand. Their son balances packed lunches on a pole. Note that this artist thought smoking quite compatible with a virtuous life.

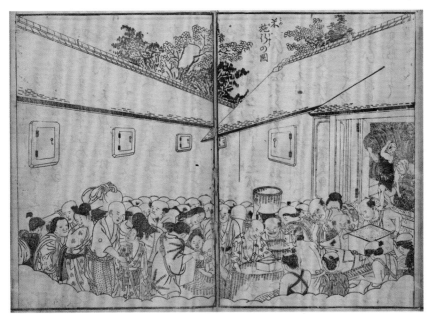

87c During a famine, Zensuke opens his granary to the poor. Rice was stored in straw bales, of the kind that a servant carries across the threshold on the right. Other servants make sure the rice is distributed fairly by measuring out a precise amount in square wooden boxes (bottom center). In the left foreground, a boy guides a blind man with a shaven head.

87d The ultimate honor: Zensuke is received by his daimyo in recognition of his charity. We see Zensuke bowing deeply while the lord (on the right, on a raised platform) speaks words of praise. We may assume that the two attendants will close the sliding doors again once the audience has ended. Zensuke would only have heard the lord's voice, but not seen his face. Shogun and daimyo alike used this technique to heighten their aura of authority. Note the grave faces on this happy occasion. Artists and early photographers rarely show smiling samurai.

87e Zensuke's eldest son, dressed as a samurai in spite of his father's humble beginnings, at his wedding ceremony. We see the bride seal the bond by drinking saké (rice wine) from a shallow cup. In an alcove behind them stands a statue of the Daoist immortal Fukurokuju. Other longevity symbols abound. Behind the carving, there is a painted scroll with cranes and pines. At the center of the ceremony, the family has placed an auspicious model landscape (shimadai): under the pines and plum blossoms of the magic isle of Hōrai, two white-haired deities rake in happiness and sweep away malice.

87f Now old and wealthy, Zensuke and his wife enjoy the view of their Japanese garden, while servants sweep, prune, weed, and bring refreshments.

87g "The End": Zensuke gives his children a scroll painting by which to remember him, bare-chested and with a hoe in hand.

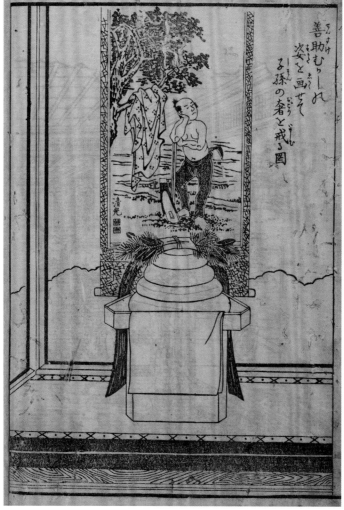

The Naughty Life

87h The wives of Itarō and his brothers engage in idle gossip at home. This artist clearly does not approve of tea parties.

87i A doctor mixes a poison that will end the pregnancy of Itarō's wife ...

87j ... as well as, very nearly, her own life. Here she is shown writhing in pain, while the quack administers more drugs and her sisters-in-law try to help. For the first time in years, the swine brothers and their wives now remember their faith. In an alcove, a little *zushi* shrine houses a Buddhist statue. What ultimately saves the woman is a sacred amulet generously donated by a neighbor. We see that paper amulet, rather exaggerated in size, on the little table. The scroll draped over its edge reads, "I put my faith in Amida," the Buddha of Infinite Light.

87k A midwife in the same village kills a child at birth. An anatomical detail leaves no doubt that the child is a boy—infanticide in Japan did not target girls alone. A folding screen delineates a protected "women-only" space in which the mother has given birth. The big basin is filled with warm water. Had it been allowed to live, the newborn would have been bathed here. Note the fiery wisp on the left page—evil karma rising from the scene of the crime. It is no coincidence that this scene is depicted so gruesomely: the intent of this book was to convince people that infanticide was a bad thing.

87l A mother, probably Itarō's wife or a sister-in-law, kills her newborn child on the floor of the birthing space. The artist is unsubtle about the implications of this act: she now has horns, a wild mane, and a demon's face.

87m The midwife is brought to trial before a magistrate. In reality, this almost never happened. Many Japanese lords banned infanticide, required women to register their pregnancies, and paid subsidies to parents with more than two or three children. But very few people were ever punished for infanticide.

87n The End, 1: The King of Hell, dressed like a Chinese magistrate, tries Itarō and his wife.

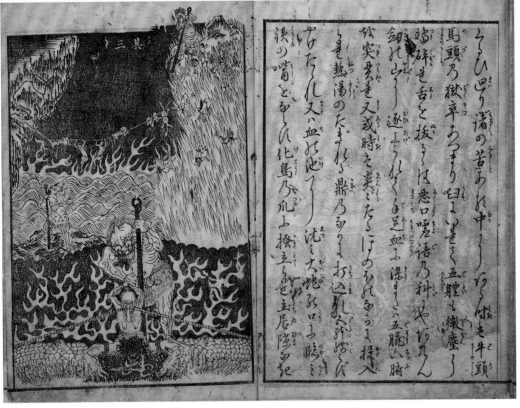

87o The End, 2: The midwife has also gone to hell, where an army of infants—her many victims over a long professional career—tears her asunder in a terrible tug-of-war.

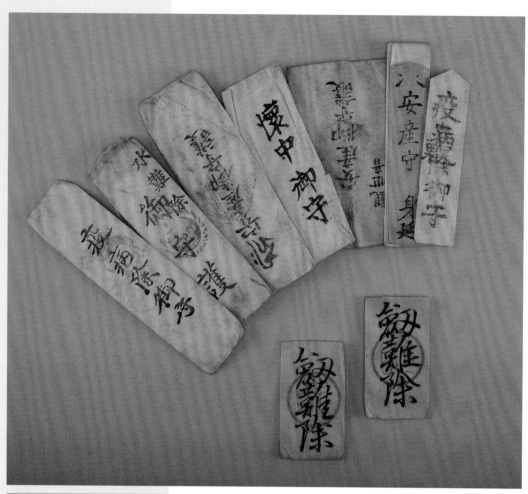

88 Amulet bundle

Some people carried entire bundles of talismans; in this collection, we see several safe-birth charms.

Warding Off Calamity

These little paper amulets grant us a poignant glimpse into the worries and fears of the people of Tokugawa Japan. Women armed themselves against difficult births with amulets, and hoped that other paper slips would preserve their children from smallpox and measles.

Amulets were commonly sold by temples and shrines, and could be potent souvenirs for pilgrims to bring home to their friends and neighbors. That they weighed next to nothing made them attractive for the average Tokugawa tourist, a pedestrian in straw sandals.

89 An amulet for safe childbirth (*Anzan-mamori*)

Maternal mortality was lower in Tokugawa Japan than in many parts of Europe, where doctors and their unwashed hands often did more harm than good. Still, giving birth was dangerous; a woman who gave birth five times over her life had a one in twenty chance of dying in childbirth.

The Quest for Longevity

Samurai idealized indifference in the face of death, and samurai and farmers alike hoped for a serene afterlife as ancestral deities. However, many Japanese also celebrated a long life in this world as a highly desirable achievement.

It was Daoism, a tradition of philosophy and magic originally formulated in China, that gave this yearning its particular shape, with its symbols of longevity (pines, cranes, and tortoises) and myths of men who transformed themselves into immortals through ascetic practice.

90 Fukurokuju, a Daoist Immortal and God of Good Fortune

This playful woodcarving on an ivory base looks like a tortoise from one side, but when turned over it reveals itself as Fukurokuju, a Daoist immortal and one of the Seven Gods of Fortune of Japanese mythology. Fukurokuju, easily identified by his distinctive elongated forehead, is the god of happiness, fortune, and longevity. The tortoise, too, is a symbol of long life and good fortune.

This print—most likely originally contained within a larger album—features a scene with several symbols of celebration and longevity: a pine tree, plum blossoms, cranes, tortoises, and bamboo leaves. The text at top presents the lyrics to a celebratory song:

In a realm at peace,	*Tenga taihei*
where the emperor	*chōkyū ni*
reigns eternal,	*osamaru miyo no*
like the wind in the pines,	*matsukaze*
young cranes	*hinazuru wa*
live for a thousand years	*chitose furu*
and in the valley streams	*tani no nagare ni*
the tortoises play	*kame asobu*

91 A Realm at Peace
Tenga taihei
(Likely early 19th century)

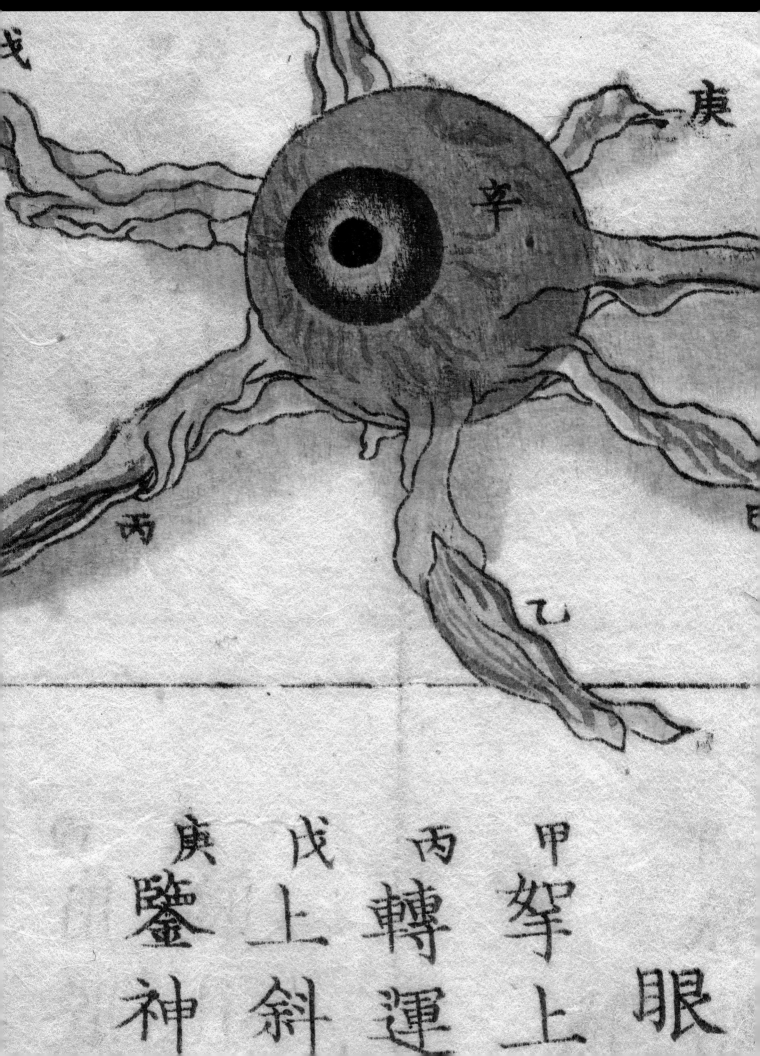

戊

庚

辛

丙

乙

丙

甲　　丙　　戊　　庚
挈　　轉　　上　　鑒
眼　　運　　斜　　神

9

Forbidden Waters and Foreign Knowledge

Between the 1630s and the 1850s, Japan's rulers made foreign travel a capital crime and limited foreign merchants (Dutch and Chinese) to two tightly controlled quarters in Nagasaki, a port city in Japan's southwest. For generations, historians lamented that this "closed country" policy arrested Japan's development.

Today, however, we pay much more attention to the many ways in which Japan continued to interact with the wider world. One of the most interesting is the sparkling curiosity with which Japanese scholars delved into Chinese and European learning, whether writing elegant poems in Chinese, diligently studying Chinese medicine, or torturously teaching themselves Dutch in order to decipher books on anatomy or physics. And scholars were not the only ones interested in the outside world. Curiosity spilled into popular culture, as well. Japan was at once closed and open.

Opposite:
92   Detail from
A New Book of Eye Medicine
Ganka shinsho
(1812–1813)

93 The Great Martyrdom of Nagasaki
Painted in Macao by an anonymous Japanese artist between 1626 and 1632

On September 10, 1622, by order of shogun Tokugawa Hidetada, 55 foreign missionaries and Japanese converts suffered martyrdom in Nagasaki. An anonymous Japanese artist, presumably a Christian convert himself, made this painting sometime in the next decade during exile in Macao.

The Suppression of Christianity

Catholic missionaries arrived in Japan in 1548 and won hundreds of thousands of converts in the following decades. Upon unifying Japan, however, the Tokugawa shoguns grew more and more mistrustful of this foreign faith whose leadership (the Pope of Rome) they could not control. By 1640 the shoguns had expelled or martyred the foreign missionaries, and forced all subjects to choose between death and apostasy. The Great Peace was not a time of religious freedom. For 240 years, all Japanese subjects had to prove that they were not adherents of the "evil teaching" (*jakyō*), as Christianity became known.

94 A cross of the hidden Christians

Some Japanese Christians clung to their faith after it was banned. For these "Hidden Christians," the ambiguity of an object like this cross gave them the hope of plausible deniability should they be discovered. Seen from one side, it is a Catholic cross. Turn it over, and a buddha sits at its center.

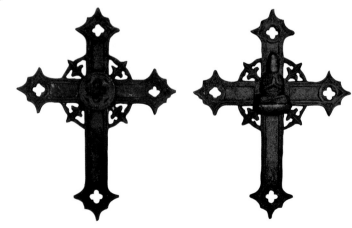

95 Register of
religious surveillance
*Kirishitan sensaku
shūmon aratamechō*
(Kamijōarai village, 1666)

This population register records the name and age of each person
in a village in the mountain basin of Kai, due west of Edo. The seals
show that a Buddhist priest has certified each villager as not being a
Christian. Today such registers have an unexpected use: they allow
historical demographers to find out when people were married, how
many children they raised, and how long they lived.

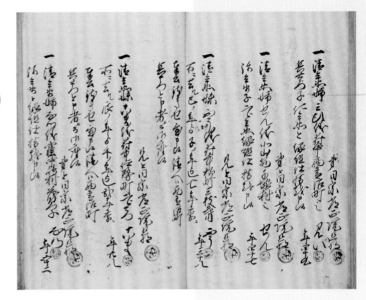

Discovering Europe, Studying China

Through the Dutch trading post and the Chinese quarter at Nagasaki Harbor, the Japanese of the
Tokugawa period had their window onto the outside world. Year in and year out, ships from China
and the Netherlands sailed into the harbor bearing their cargoes: silk thread, textiles, medicines, sugar,
dyes, scientific instruments, clocks, and more.

But among their most important cargo were people and books. Scholars came to Nagasaki from across
Japan to study the Dutch and vernacular Chinese languages, to acquire rare and useful imported
books, and to gain knowledge of medicine and other fields through firsthand exchanges.

96 *Illustrations of
Strange Diseases and
Their Surgical Treatments
Kishitsu geryō zukan*
(Undated hand copy)

Before the invention of anesthesia, undergoing surgery was a horrific
proposition. Surgeons had to cut and sew under extreme time
pressure, making many life-saving interventions impossible. In the
West, the first successful operations under general anesthesia took
place in Boston in 1846. But in Japan, this milestone was passed in
1804 by a determined Japanese doctor and his creative merging of
Western and Chinese medical knowledge.

The physician Hanaoka Seishū (1760–1835) studied with Japanese
experts in both European surgery and traditional Chinese medicine.
Hanaoka was inspired by the example of a legendary Chinese doctor
who claimed to have anesthetized patients in the second century CE.
But since that doctor burned his own books, Hanaoka had to start
his research from scratch. Through years of experiments conducted
on his wife and his mother, he arrived at an effective formula for
anesthesia that incorporated various Chinese medicinal plants. The
first of many patients to benefit from his innovation was a 60-year-
old woman whose breast cancer he resected.

This success came at a price: Hanaoka's mother died from one
experimental potion, and his wife lost her eyesight from another.

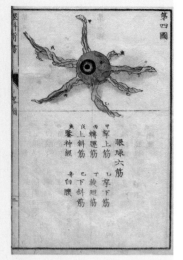

*97 A New Book
of Eye Medicine
Ganka shinsho
(1812–1813)*

Two centuries ago, European medicine could present grave dangers to patients. But it also impressed Japanese physicians with its achievements, especially in the fields of anatomy and surgery. Unlocking this knowledge from afar often required enormous efforts.

In 1794 the shogunal physician Katsuragawa Hoshū (1754–1809) obtained from the Dutch traders visiting Edo a Dutch-language translation of Joseph Plenck's ophthalmological treatise *Doctrina de Morbis Oculorum* (1782). The painstaking process of deciphering the original and devising appropriate Japanese translations for specialized terminology took nearly two decades to complete. The finished product was a milestone in the early modern Japanese encounter with Western medicine and features striking color illustrations by the Western-style artist Ishikawa Tairō (1765–1817). This image shows the eyeball and its six extraocular muscles.

Foreign Knowledge Presented and Parodied

Various Tales from the Dutch is a collection of several dozen short essays on the Dutch and Western knowledge that was widely read in the late Tokugawa period.

The entries range broadly across European customs, scientific knowledge, and material culture. The topics discussed include Western cuisine, disease, funerary customs, hospitals, asbestos, homosexuality, mummies, crocodiles, lions, electricity, speaking-trumpets (bullhorns), fountains, and Western drawing techniques. The page shown here depicts the recent advent of lighter-than-air travel.

Morishima Chūryō, the work's author, was also an active writer of fiction. Among his many works is the comic-book parody of *Chūshingura* on the opposite page, the title of which replaces *chūshin* ("loyal retainers") with *Tōjin*, a term used in reference to Chinese people and foreigners generally. As this substitution suggests, the story humorously reimagines the events of the original play through the incorporation of foreign learning and items of imported material culture.

Many of these items had been introduced nine years earlier in *Various Tales from the Dutch*.

*98 Various Tales from the Dutch
Kōmō zatsuwa
(1787)*

Various Tales from the Dutch includes this illustration of an airship. The accompanying discussion is remarkably up to date, as the first lighter-than-air flights had taken place in Europe less than four years earlier.

*A Foreign-Themed Parody
of Chūshingura
Karadehon Tōjingura
(1796)*

99a   Much of the comic-book's action revolves around the frantic efforts of the 47 ronin to procure items for a large-scale exhibition of exotic artifacts. The tableau here (top) corresponds to a scene in *Chūshingura* in which one of the loyal retainers, mistakenly believing himself to have murdered his father-in-law, takes his own life. Here he is seen asking his companions to mummify his body and use it as his entry for the exhibition.

Embedded in the scene is a humorous allusion to a celebrated moment in the history of Western medicine in Japan. The onlooker at upper right is seen comparing the real-life organs with those on an anatomical chart. A similar comparison of a dissected prisoner's body with Western anatomical illustrations had prompted several Japanese physicians to undertake the first translation of a Western anatomical treatise two decades earlier. Adding another layer of humor, the chart unfurled in the image is in the style of Chinese anatomical charts, not Western ones.

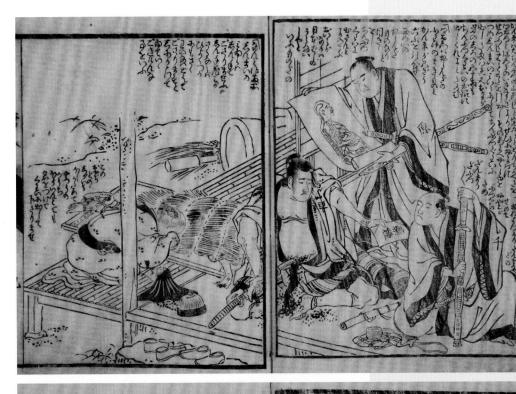

99b   The illustration here parodies the famous seventh act of *Chūshingura*, in which the head retainer Yuranosuke feigns dissolution in the pleasure quarters of Kyoto. Aside from the use of a magnifying lens (upper right) and eyeglasses (bottom), the most striking element in the scene is the airship at upper left, aboard which Yuranosuke's son hurries home after delivering the unfurled letter to his father.

10

Japan in Ainu Lands

Before the 1870s, maps of Japan typically went no farther than the southern tip of the island then called Ezo or Ezochi and now known as Hokkaido. This was the home of the Ainu, a people whose lifeways were starkly distinct from those of Japan. Speaking a separate language of their own, the Ainu lived in small communities as hunters and fishermen.

Like the American collectors whose treasures are shown here, the Ainu were drawn to the beauty of Japan's material culture. Like the American collectors, and like us, they infused Japanese artifacts—especially lacquerware—with new meanings.

Over the course of the Tokugawa period, contact with their vastly more numerous southern neighbors transformed Ainu lives for both good and ill. The Ainu became dependent partners in a trade that exchanged the animal products of their wooded homeland for Japanese manufactures, tobacco, alcohol, and rice.

Ultimately, exploitation, physical abuse, and diseases ravaged the Ainu and greatly reduced their population. By the 1880s, when the American collectors of these objects began to travel to Hokkaido, Westerners had become fascinated with the Ainu in part for their heavy beards and supposedly European facial features, and in part as one of "vanishing races" of the world. Luckily, they were not quite right: Ainu culture survives, if tenuously, to this day.

Unlike their southern neighbors, the Ainu of the 17th to 19th centuries rarely speak to us in their own voices. Instead, their lives and worldviews are refracted through the memories of their modern-day descendants and the accounts of earlier visitors from Tokugawa Japan and the West.

Opposite:
100   This lacquer drinking cup (*tuki*) with a stand was reserved for ceremonial libations. Carved by an Ainu hand, the cup may have acquired its lacquer veneer from a Japanese artisan.

101 Necklace

This necklace combines 17th-century Japan coins with glass beads that traveled to the Ainu across many thousands of miles, either on a Dutch ship from Europe and then through Japan, or from Russia or China through Sakhalin. The colors in the beads, especially the yellow glass, point to China as their most likely point of origin.

Ainu Trade

Trade linked the Ainu to both continental Asia and Japan. In the course of the Great Peace, Japanese demand for furs, feathers, marine products, and live hawks led some Ainu communities to hunt their territories to exhaustion. Trade with Japan allowed the Ainu to obtain goods they desired, including exquisite pieces of lacquer that they used as status symbols and in ceremonies. But the trade was not conducted on equal terms, and was often backed up by the threat or reality of violence. For example, when one Ainu community began to plant rice, so as not to import it any longer, the daimyo of Matsumae, whose domain lived by trading with the Ainu, dispatched his officials to uproot the young plants.

Every (Wo)Man an Artist

The Ainu divided tasks between men and women. Women made and ornamented textiles and men expressed themselves in woodcarvings. A man who courted a woman would carve a knife for her. If she was interested, she would weave and embroider a robe for him in return.

How were Ainu robes made?

Ainu robes combine cloth imported from Japan with a fabric that the Ainu produced themselves. To make that fabric (*attush*), they harvested the inner bark of trees.

After soaking for about 10 days, often in a hot spring, the fibers were soft enough to be pulled apart into strings. Women wove them into fabric on their backstrap looms.

Women embroidered these tree bark robes with patterns cut from imported Japanese hemp or cotton cloth. A woman's skill in creating these patterns was highly prized.

102 An *attush* robe (treebark fibers with indigo-dyed Japanese cloth)

Curious Sights of the Isles of Ezo
Ezo-tō kikan
(1799)

103a An Ainu man strips the inner bark of a tree, which his wife collects in a basket.

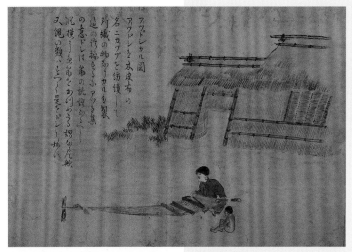

103b An Ainu woman weaves an attush tree bark fabric, while a little girl looks on.

103c An Ainu woman teaches two girls how to make textile patterns and watches as they practice with a stick in the sand.

104 *Ruunpe* robe

Most Ainu wore clothes made from tree bark with indigo-dyed cotton patterns, but communities along one part of Hokkaido's south coast also sewed very colorful patchwork robes, called *ruunpe*, entirely made from imported Japanese fabrics.

What do the designs mean?

When Ainu were asked about the meaning of their designs in the 20th century, they stressed that they do not represent animals. Drawing likenesses of animals or people was thought to trap their souls in the design, and no Ainu wanted an angry animal spirit writhing in his or her robe. When in the late 19th century, Western "explorers" and tourists made sketches of Ainu without their consent, conflicts often erupted. The Ainu felt gravely violated, while the Westerners had no sense of having wronged them.

The designs are said to be unique to each robe, but have certain commonalities within individual regions. In this sense, they may have expressed regional identities.

Why are the patterns concentrated on the hemline and sleeves?

The Ainu apparently believed that evil spirits could enter a person's body through the openings of his or her robe, especially from behind. The patterns worked as a defensive charm, protecting each of these portals, and especially the wearer's back.

105 An *attush* robe
Shown from the front (left) and back (right)

106, 107, 108, 109
Multi-purpose carving knives
(*makiri*)

Both men and women wore
these *makiri* on their belts, but
it was men who used them for
carving other knives, as well as
the smoking sets, prayer sticks,
and stylized messenger birds also
shown here.

When two Ainu men met for the first time, they would break the ice by exchanging their pipes. As they sat and puffed, they would admire the carvings on the other man's smoking kit, sizing up his carving abilities and, by extension, his worth as a man.

Like Ainu robes, smoking kits show geometric designs, but never animals, whose spirits were not to be trapped in such mundane objects.

Pipes were secured by inserting them in the socket on the pipe holder, which could then be tucked in the owner's belt. Men routinely carried these. In one Ainu tale, a man fended off a bear just with his pipe holder and tobacco box.

110 Smoking kit (*tanpakuop*), consisting of a pipe holder and a tobacco box

111 Pipe

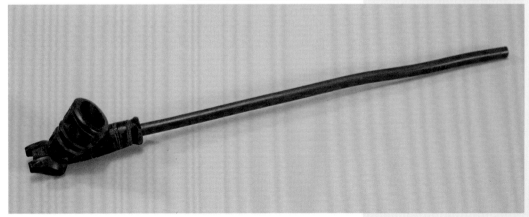

112, 113, 114 Ikupasuy: Sacred wands or "moustache lifters"?

Carved Prayers

The fascination with Ainu beards has colored the interpretation of the *ikupasuy* (prayer stick). Already in a Japanese survey of the peoples of the world (real as well as imagined) printed in 1799, the ikupasuy helps a hairy Ainu man to keep his bushy beard from dropping into his drink. In fact, ikupasuy feature in the very first appearance of Ainu in a Western source. Luís Fróis had just arrived in Kyoto as a Jesuit missionary when, in 1565, he came across a delegation of Ainu men. He described them as "savage men, clothed in beastes skynnes, rough bodyed, with huge beardes, and monstruous muchaches, the which they hold up with little forkes as they drynk" (English translation published in London in 1577).

Although Ainu men did touch their moustaches with ikupasuy, the real function of these objects was to serve as a vehicle for prayers. Before drinking saké, they would dip their ikupasuy and sprinkle some drops as an offering to the gods, either on their head and back, or onto the stylized birds made from shaved tree branches, or *inaw* (opposite). Each Ainu man carved his own prayer stick, and each prayer stick bears a unique design. This was more than an expression of individual spirituality: the ikupasuy identified the worshipper before the gods. As a sacred object, prayer sticks sometimes featured carvings of animals, whose spirits could serve as messengers.

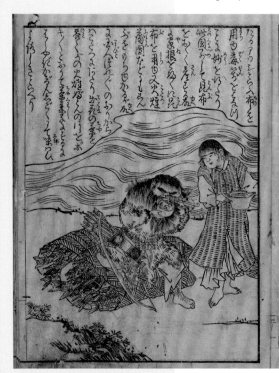

Illustrated Overview of Strange Lands
Ehon ikoku ichiran
(1799)

115 Japanese and Westerners have long been fascinated with Ainu beards. They made for a contrast with the smooth cheeks of many Japanese men, but have often been grotesquely exaggerated in Tokugawa-period illustrations, to the point of giving the representations of Ainu men an animal-like appearance.

The Ainu believed that their prayers could not reach the land of the gods (*kamuy mosir*) directly. During prayers, men dipped an ikupasuy in saké and sprinkled it over the inaw. The inaw would then take flight as a bird, bearing the message to the intended deity.

Inaw come in an intricate variety of designs, since each god had his own shape and material. Each inaw was intended for a single use only; once it had delivered its prayer, it lost its power.

The Ainu also placed inaw in their homes and on the graves of their dead.

116b   An Ainu cemetery

116a   Inaw were carved by stripping and tufting thin layers of bark from a tree branch, as in this illustration from *Curious Sights of the Isles of Ezo*.

117   Stylized birds bearing a prayer (*inaw*)

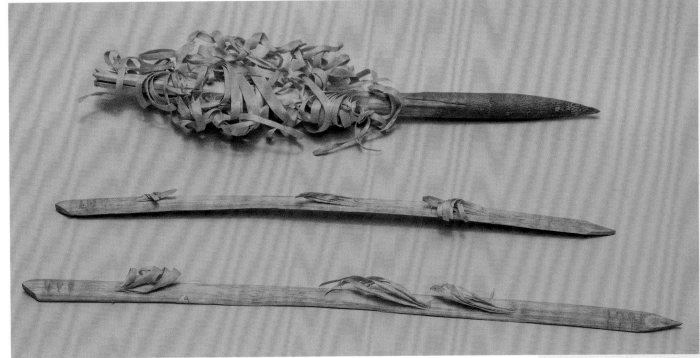

97

Visiting Gods and Japanese Treasure: The Bear-Sending Ceremony

The Ainu believed that they and their gods usually lived in separate worlds. When the gods wanted to visit, they cloaked themselves in the body of an animal and waited for the Ainu to catch it. Such was the case with bear cubs, which the Ainu sometimes took from their mothers and raised in wooden cages in their villages, a furry god in their midst. Sometimes the bear was even fed human breast milk. After about a year, the villagers would help the god return to his own world—by ritually killing the young bear. They then placed its corpse in a sacred enclosure and surrounded it with the greatest treasures of the community.

In all depictions of this ceremony that have come down to us, these treasures are overwhelmingly of Japanese manufacture. As we have seen in earlier chapters, swords and lacquerware served as status symbols within Japan. The Ainu, too, used them as markers of rank and wealth, but in addition employed them as sacred ritual objects.

Curious Sights of the Isles of Ezo shows us glimpses of the Ainu through Japanese eyes. The author, Murakami Shimanojō (also known as Hata Awagimaru), was a skilled land surveyor and mapmaker from Ise in central Japan. In 1798 the shogunate dispatched him to the islands of Ezo (including the Kuriles, now under Russian control). After about a year of walking among Ainu communities there, he wrote and illustrated this book, in part to create a record of what he even then feared were the vanishing lifeways of the Ainu. His original drawings were copied many times and inspired other "Ainu pictures," some by artists who had never seen an Ainu in the flesh.

118a Ainu men carve inaw in preparation for a bear-sending ceremony. Nearby, a dance circles around the wooden cage in which the community has reared the bear cub.

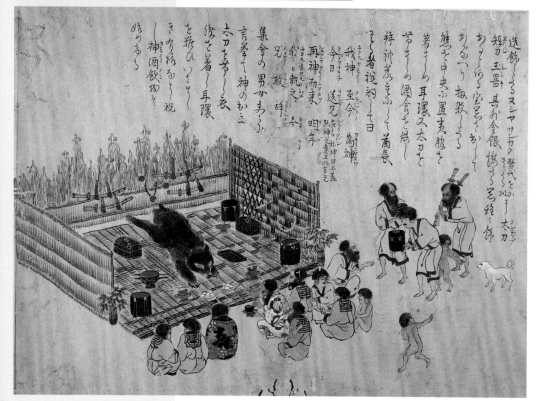

118b In the bear-sending ceremony (*iyomante*), an Ainu community takes leave of a bear cub it has raised and ritually killed. They arrange treasures around the body: necklaces of imported glass, Japanese swords, and especially a variety of Japanese lacquer containers. At the back of the enclosure a flock of inaw awaits to carry prayers to the land of the gods. One man, facing the bear, is about to sprinkle saké from a tuki cup with his prayer stick.

The Ainu and Japanese Lacquerware

By the 18th century, Japanese lacquer was synonymous with treasure (*ikor*) among the Ainu. Some Ainu owned lacquer of inferior quality, which they may have used as functional containers and utensils. But at least some Ainu were keen connoisseurs of maki-e lacquer: one is on record as having exchanged five bear skins for a single beautiful vessel.

In the various production centers of Japan, artisans made lacquer objects for export to the Ainu, but some lacquerware was also sold secondhand to the Ainu, who paid higher prices for old vessels than did the Japanese. It is said (but to our knowledge not well documented) that even some treasures from daimyo collections found their way into Ainu villages, as daimyo houses fell under fiscal strain or simply decided that their great-great-great-grandmother's trousseau was taking up too much space in storage. The large bowl shown below may well be one such case.

119 The lacquerware items below are the same pictured in this photograph by collector Mabel Loomis Todd.

120, 121, 122, 123
Left to right: Lacquer food bowl, lacquer teapot, round lacquer box, and shell game box.

11

The Opening of Japan, the Closing of the Great Peace

Tokugawa Japan was no stagnant society. But in the absence of war, its military technology changed relatively little. As stipulated by the maritime bans of the 1630s, its ships remained small and designed for coastal trade. In the 1630s, the shogun commanded as many guns as any ruler in Europe, but by the early 1850s samurai swords and muskets looked quaint and historic to Western eyes.

In July 1853, a fleet of American warships sailed and steamed into Edo Bay, demanding that Japan open for trade. One month later, a Russian expedition entered Nagasaki Harbor bearing a similar message. After some hesitation, the shogun gradually opened Japan to foreign visitors.

This concession undermined the shogunate's authority within Japan. In 1868, a coalition of southwestern domains marched on Edo with the 15-year-old emperor as their figurehead. The last shogun surrendered the great city without a fight, even though his war chest was full and many tens of thousands of samurai remained under his command. In China, the cataclysmic Taiping Wars (1850–1864) had just cost between 20 and 100 million lives, and in the United States, an entire generation of young men had bled on the battlefields of the Civil War (1861–1865). The last ruler of the Tokugawa line evidently felt it more important for Japan to be united and at peace than for him to remain its ruler.

The new government claimed to restore an ancient order in which an emperor, descended from the sun goddess, had both reigned and ruled. Although many of the insurgents had been rabid xenophobes, intent on expelling every last foreigner from the "divine country" of Japan, the new government continued and then greatly intensified the shogunate's policies of adopting technologies, institutions, and ideas from the West.

The agents of this revolution were overwhelmingly samurai, many of them ambitious young men from the lower ranks. Yet within a few years of seizing power, they abolished the privileges of the samurai and forbade anyone who was not a policeman or an officer in the new army to wear swords in public. In a sense, the samurai abolished themselves.

This was the Meiji period. It was an age of discovery and dynamism, of nation building and industrialization, and also of new foreign wars. The Great Peace of the shoguns was over.

Opposite:
124 Silk purse with ornaments repurposed from sword scabbard (Late 19th century, Meiji period)

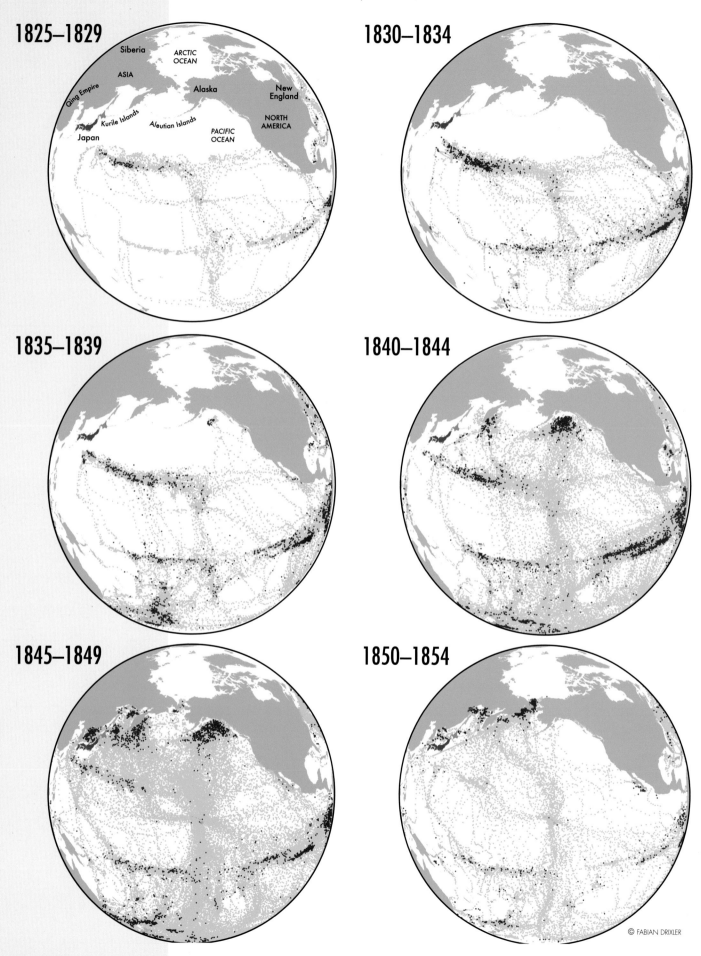

1825–1829

Siberia
ARCTIC
OCEAN
ASIA
Qing Empire
Alaska
New
England
Kurile Islands
Aleutian Islands
NORTH
AMERICA
Japan
PACIFIC
OCEAN

1830–1834

1835–1839

1840–1844

1845–1849

1850–1854

© FABIAN DRIXLER

The World Hunt

While Tokugawa Japan built its civilization on the limited resources of its archipelago, the nations of the West reached out across the world. By the 1850s, both Russian and American ships had closed in on Japan, two great arms of what environmental historians now call "the world hunt."

In 1800, the North Pacific still teemed with fur-bearing animals and whales. Russian trappers, moving across Siberia into the Kuriles, Aleutians, and Alaska, caught sea otters and other mammals for sale to Europe and especially to China. A limited number of English whalers operated in sight of Japan's shores by the 1820s, and even made occasional contact with local Japanese fishermen. American whalers, mostly from New England, expanded their hunting grounds into the Pacific in the 1820s, moved toward Japan in the 1830s, and in the 1840s swarmed out across the entire North Pacific. Finding Japanese ports where whalers could resupply was a high priority for the United States government, but Japan's official policy at the time was to "shell and repel" foreign ships "without a second thought."

The U.S. global whale catch peaked just before Commodore Matthew Perry's American flotilla entered Edo Bay in 1853. About a decade later, kerosene emerged as a cheaper substitute for whale oil. American whaling continued into the 20th century, but never again approached the economic and political prominence it had held around 1850.

126 Whale vertebra

Opposite:
125 The daily positions of whaling vessels when whales were and were not reported killed, based on a large sample of logbooks from American whaling ships. The data were assembled between 2000 and 2010 during the Census of Marine Life project (www.coml.org) by Tim D. Smith, Randall R. Reeves, Elizabeth A. Josephson, and Judith N. Lund, who made them available for the purpose of creating these maps.

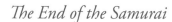

127, 128 Tokugawa Yoshinobu, the last shogun, in Western military attire and in formal Japanese dress.

129, 130, 131 Samurai sword scabbard ornaments (*menuki*). *Counterclockwise from left*: A seated man, a pin with floral decoration, and a fish.

The Closing of the Great Peace

In many histories of Japan, the shogunate is portrayed as hopelessly conservative compared to the modernizing spirit of the Meiji government that replaced it. In fact, the shogunate enacted several reforms during its last years and embraced certain aspects of Western culture.

Here we see the last shogun, Tokugawa Yoshinobu, moving with apparent ease between the two worlds. In the spring of 1867, the camera captured him in the kind of outfit that his predecessors had worn for many generations. In 1866 or 1867, he also posed for a portrait in a French-style uniform with a European saber. Nobody knew it then, but within a decade the age of the samurai would be over, and neither samurai swords nor samurai topknots would be seen on Japan's streets.

The End of the Samurai

It does not happen often in world history that a ruling class abolishes itself, but the samurai had better reasons than most. However fascinated we are with them today, the lives of most samurai were stifled by tedious rituals and impoverished by the expenses of their status, such as largely ornamental servants and oversized houses. By the mid-19th century, most samurai held the same rank and position that their great-great-great-great-great-great-great-great-great grandfathers (adopted or real) had occupied.

By losing their privileges and guaranteed incomes, the samurai also shed old burdens and gained new opportunities. The time of the samurai was over.

American Tourists and Collectors

As the Meiji period unfolded, European and American merchants, foreign experts, and tourists traveled all over Japan in growing numbers. Drawn to the beauty of Japanese artifacts and fascinated with a half-mythologized image of the samurai, they bought folding screens and woodblock prints, lacquerware and porcelain, bright swords and fierce-looking armor. When they returned home, they impressed their friends in parlors festooned in the material culture of the Tokugawa period.

Among the purchases of the American collectors were the heirlooms of houses old in honor but now short on liquidity. In other cases, families still wealthy divested of collectibles that had lost their cultural function in the new world of the Meiji period. Among Japan's elites, now wearing frock coats and sending their sons to Oxford and Paris, Berlin and New Haven, displaying armor, swords, and expensive lacquer dowries was no longer an important way to show off their status.

132, 133   Collector Mabel Loomis Todd in about 1907 and in Japan in 1896, posing in a kimono.

134   Purse with ivory button and ornament repurposed from sword scabbard (Late 19th century, Meiji period)

So large was the demand in the West that Japanese artisans produced items specifically for a Western audience. These whimsical inrō may or may not have been fashioned with Western buyers in mind. The sword (*katana*) below, of lesser quality than the others in the Yale Peabody Museum collection, was made as a tourist trinket. Old samurai blades, meanwhile, were no longer worn in public and sometimes had the precious metals of their scabbards quarried for their ornaments. In an act of unintended poetry, sword fittings have been repurposed as decoration for two charming purses shown in this chapter, while other ornaments were fashioned into jewelry pins.

135 Black lacquer inrō
With ivory netsuke in the shape of a theater mask, and ivory ojime

136 Lacquer inrō
With ivory netsuke and gold and silver ojime

138 Lacquer writing box
with implements
(Late 19th century,
Meiji period)

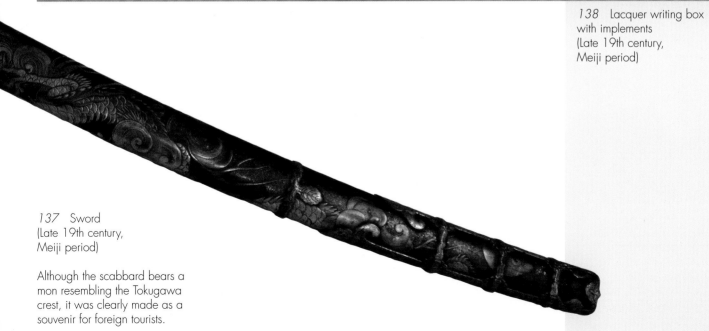

137 Sword
(Late 19th century,
Meiji period)

Although the scabbard bears a
mon resembling the Tokugawa
crest, it was clearly made as a
souvenir for foreign tourists.

The Yale Collectors

Most of the objects exhibited in *Samurai and the Culture of Japan's Great Peace* are from Yale's own collections, and were acquired by collectors with Yale affiliations. Some were purchased during trips to Japan in the late 19th and early 20th centuries, whereas others were bought by agents in Japan or from dealers in the United States. This chapter offers some biographical details about these collectors and their objects.

Swords

Five swords from Yale collectors are featured in the exhibition. The first (*4*), which dates from the 15th century, was acquired in Japan by **Henry Walcott Farnam** (1853–1933, Yale College 1874) on his 1890–1891 around-the-world honeymoon. Farnam was a professor of economics at the

Shepherd Stevens and his "auntie" Charlotte Davenport in early September 1903.

Photographic print, Shepherd Stevens Papers (MS 865), Manuscripts & Archives, Yale University Library

former Sheffield Scientific School (SSS) at Yale and also served as University treasurer. His father, Henry Farnam (1803–1883), had made his fortune engineering, building, and operating canals and railroads in Connecticut, as well as the Chicago, Rock Island, and Pacific Railroad in the Midwest. The Farnams were generous benefactors of the University, and their former home on Hillhouse Avenue is now the President's House.

Two of the Peabody's swords (*13, 14*) were given by **Evelyn Sloane Griswold** (d. 1944), wife of William E. S. Griswold (1876–1964, YC 1899). These were acquired by her father, John Sloane, who for many years was the president of W. & J. Sloane, the New York importer of rugs and antiques. In 1912, Griswold's uncles, William Douglas Sloane (YC 1866) and Henry Thompson Sloane (YC 1868), funded the construction of the Sloane Physics Laboratory, an active research and teaching facility on Prospect Street.

The final pair of swords (*18, 19*) was purchased by **Shepherd Stevens** (1880–1962) and donated to the Peabody Museum in 1949. Stevens was raised from the age of eight by his "auntie" Charlotte and uncle William Davenport. On his graduation from Columbia University in 1903, Charlotte treated her nephew to a voyage around the world. Departing from San Francisco, they arrived in Yokohama in late July for what was to be a two-month stay in Japan.

Stevens's diaries from the trip are extensive and candid, and written in an easily legible hand that shows evidence of his architectural training at Columbia. He describes the purchase of the swords from an antique dealer named Hayashi as follows:

> Stopped in before tiffin at Hayashi's, spent nearly an hour looking at swords and sword-hilts, of which I had quite an array spread out on the floor. Bought a hilt (stork, with outstretched wing, 1½ yen) and a pair of swords, one short and one long, with handsome green lacquered (ground shell) scabbards and the usual sharkskin handles. On the blades up in the handle, are the name of the maker, Nagamichi of the province Oshu, and the "year-name"; Bun-kyū -garnem [*sic*, i.e. *Bunkyū gannen*, or 1861] [...]. They were 6½ yen—quite cheap it seems to me. (August 22, 1903)

Stevens's travels included a week in the area around Nikkō, home to the mausoleums of the Tokugawa shoguns Ieyasu and Iemitsu. The weather was quite hot, and while hiking alone he often went skinny-dipping, as his diary relates with evident glee. Stevens also offers humorous commentary on the stifling attire of visiting Americans, as compared to the more comfortable cotton garments of the Japanese. He admits that he himself often went without underwear beneath his white linen suits— one of which we see him wearing in the accompanying photograph.

Stevens went on to travel extensively both at home and in Europe. He continued his architectural studies and earned a degree from the École des Beaux Arts in Paris in 1908. After some years in business, followed by service in World War I, he assumed an academic appointment first at Cornell University, then at Yale in 1920. He remained at Yale until his retirement in 1947 and funded a visiting professorship at the Yale School of Architecture in honor of his aunt and uncle.

Books

A number of the Tokugawa-period books in the exhibition were donated to the University by Yale faculty members. Such is the case with *The Iroha Library* (*Iroha bunko*, 1836–1872 [*67a, 67b, 67c*]), the popular account of the 47 ronin that was translated into English by Shiuichiro Saito and Edward Greey in 1880. Yale's Sterling Memorial Library houses two nearly complete sets of the original Japanese edition, one of which was bought with money donated in 1873 by paleontology professor **Othniel Charles Marsh** (1831–1899, YC 1860, Ph.D. 1862), who was also the unofficial first director of the Peabody Museum (and original purchaser of the so-called "urchin man" suit of armor [*40, 41*]).

Marsh's gift of $500 allowed the university librarian, **Addison Van Name** (1835–1922, YC 1858, M.A. 1861), to purchase some 2,700 volumes from Japan. Although Saito and Greey relied mainly on a copy from a Boston collector named Gilbert Attwood, they are also known to have borrowed works by Tamenaga Shunsui (the author of the first volumes of *The Iroha Library*) from the Yale collection. It is not implausible, then, that they consulted the Yale copy in the course of preparing their translation.

Van Name had been appointed instructor in Hebrew in 1861, and in addition was an active student of Arabic, Chinese, and Japanese. He was named university librarian in 1865. Two years later he married Julia Gibbs, the sister of his Yale classmate and renowned physicist Josiah Willard Gibbs (1839–1903, YC 1858, Ph.D. 1863). In the decades that followed, Van Name built Yale's Japanese collection into one of the finest in the United States and assembled a sizable personal collection, as well.

In 1907, the Japanese collection entered another period of expansion under its new curator, **Asakawa Kan'ichi** (1873–1948, Ph.D. 1903), who joined the University faculty that year. It was also that year that the second set of *The Iroha Library* entered the library collection. In 1920, Van Name donated more than 300 of his own Japanese and Chinese books to the library, among them the copy of Shikitei Sanba's *Illustrated Encyclopedia of the Theater* (*Shibai kinmōzui*, 1803 [*64, 70a, 70b*]).

Mabel Loomis Todd and Millicent Todd Bingham in 1931, working on letters on the porch of their home on Hog Island, Maine.

Photographic print, Todd-Bingham Picture Collection, 1837–1966 (inclusive), Manuscripts & Archives, Yale University Library, digital image 10482

Lacquerware and Art Objects

Through the donations of a diverse group of men and women, the Peabody Museum has built a small but attractive collection of lacquerware and other art objects. **Thomas Sedgwick Van Volkenburgh** (1843–1921, YC 1866) probably never traveled to Japan himself, but he was an extremely good customer of the famous New York and Boston dealer Yamanaka & Company and built an extensive collection of Japanese lacquer boxes and inrō. **William Michael Zumbro** (1865–1922, Divinity School 1893) acquired the noh mask [59] representing *shōjō*, the water sprite, en route back to his mission in India in 1907.

Elizabeth Lauder Kellum (1883–1930) was the youngest child of George Lauder—a cousin of Andrew Carnegie—and his wife Anna Maria. While sailing the Pacific in 1924 and 1925, Elizabeth acquired a multitude of artifacts, including two exquisite gold lacquer boxes (*43, 44, 48*) that came to the Peabody in 1932.

The story surrounding this acquisition is one of wealth, love, and heartbreak. The Lauders spent their winters in lower Florida, where from 1907 George chartered a boat for tarpon fishing captained by Medford R. Kellum (1874–1934). For the next three years, Kellum ardently courted the young heiress Elizabeth, and in 1910 the two were secretly married. When the bride's parents found out, they were not pleased.

For some time afterward, Kellum enjoyed financial success in the Florida real estate business. Yet he missed his days at sea, and he and Elizabeth eventually relocated to Hawaii. There he found a group of like-minded individuals at the research facility associated with the Bernice P. Bishop Museum in Honolulu. Accompanied by six museum scientists, the Kellums set out into the Pacific on their newly acquired 190-foot, four-masted schooner, the *Kaimiloa*.

Elizabeth's father had died shortly before their departure, and his feelings about her husband notwithstanding, he left her an enormous sum of money. This development may have lain behind the rumors, which began to circulate right from the start of the expedition, that a rift had developed in the marriage. These were confirmed only a few years later, in 1928, when Elizabeth filed for divorce. She passed away two years later.

Elizabeth's older sister, Harriet Lauder Greenway, whose husband was an administrator at Yale, took in Elizabeth's eight-year-old daughter. It was through Harriet's efforts that many of the artifacts Elizabeth acquired on her tour of the Pacific entered the Peabody collection.

This map of Ezo indicates the path of the total eclipse of the sun and the location of the Amherst Station in 1896. Unfortunately, the sky was overcast during the event. Again David Todd was unable to take photographs of the corona, duplicating his experience in Japan for the 1886 event.

From *Corona and Coronet*, 158

MAP OF
JAPAN
SHOWING THE TRACK OF
TOTAL SOLAR ECLIPSE
August 9th 1896

Ainu Materials

The Yale Peabody Museum's holdings of artifacts pertaining to the Ainu were built through the efforts of a number of collectors—for example, **Frank Benedict Cleland** (1874–?, SSS 1897), who obtained some of the items in this exhibition in the course of travels in Hokkaido in 1902. But many of the finest and most interesting artifacts in the Museum's Ainu collection were acquired by one woman: **Mabel Loomis Todd** (1856–1932).

In 1964, Yale received a treasure trove of manuscripts, photographs, and objects from **Millicent Todd Bingham** (1880–1968); about 2,000 of these items are now in the Peabody Museum, and the manuscripts and photographic material occupy more than 200 linear feet of shelf space in the Yale Library's Manuscript and Archives collections. This acquisition was the outcome of negotiations led by Professor of English Richard B. Sewall and assisted by archivist Judith Schiff at Sterling Memorial Library. Sewall and Schiff were eager to obtain these materials because of Mabel Loomis Todd's close connection to Emily Dickinson.

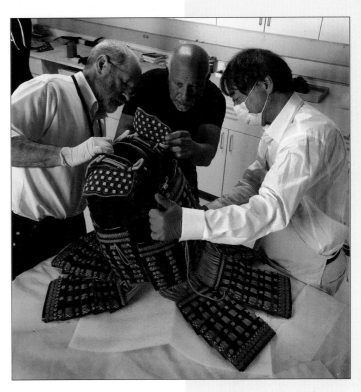

Roger Colten, Maishe Dickman and Morihiro Ogawa examine a suit of armor from the Peabody's anthropology collections.

Photograph by R. A. Kissel

Bingham was the only child of David Peck Todd (1855–1939) and Mabel Loomis Todd. Their interaction with the Dickinson family of Amherst is famous and was a source of scandal at the time. Mabel Todd was a painter, talented writer, charismatic lecturer, and the first editor of Emily Dickinson's poetry. David Todd, a professor at Amherst College, was an accomplished designer of astronomical instruments, and he often led expeditions to photograph the corona of the sun during total eclipses. Mabel regularly accompanied him on these trips and reported on her adventures around the globe for American audiences.

In advance of their second scientific expedition to Japan, undertaken to observe the total eclipse of August 7, 1896, Mabel consulted with Edward Sylvester Morse, the director of the Peabody Essex Museum in Salem, who had spent many years in Japan collecting art and artifacts. Although she was unable to persuade him to join the voyage, Morse prepped Todd on the Ainu and commissioned her to purchase artifacts for his museum.

In the course of her 10-day stay, Todd rode many miles on horseback visiting scattered Ainu villages and homes. For more than a century, the Ainu had acquired Japanese lacquerware in exchange for the fish, seaweed, animal pelts, and other goods they provided Japanese traders. As Todd later recalled, word spread quickly of her efforts to acquire lacquer and other Ainu objects:

> The Ainu near Esashi had quite taken me to their innocent hearts, and every day some of them came with one thing or another, learning that I really enjoyed their utensils and ornaments. When an old woman appeared at the eclipse station carrying one of their greatly valued round lacquer boxes, with permission for me to buy it, I felt that I had really won their affection.

Todd was so pleased with her acquisitions that she included a photograph (*119*), in which we can see this very lacquer box (*24, 27, 120*), in the book recounting her Japan trip. Morse's principal commission—to acquire an Ainu ornamental robe and boots fabricated from salmon skin—was successfully executed later that month.

Acknowledgments

Although three names appear on the cover, this book is the result of many people's creativity and dedication.

Beginning in 2013, a formidable team at the Yale Peabody Museum of Natural History developed *Samurai and the Culture of Japan's Great Peace* as a special exhibition. Laura Friedman translated the story into a three-dimensional design. David Heiser provided pedagogical insight. Sally Pallatto led the exhibition's graphic design, designed the catalog, and coordinated photography; its beauty is a testament to her skills and those of Rosemary Volpe, who directed the book's production, assisted by Stacy Murray and Catherine Walters. Annette Van Aken coordinated object loans and permissions. Harry Shyket provided technical expertise. Maishe Dickman manufactured artifact mounts, and the exhibition was constructed by Michael Anderson, Walter Brenckle, Robert Charlesworth, and John Ferro. For her logistical support, we also thank Bonnie Mahmood. This exhibition would have been impossible without Roger H. Colten, Senior Collections Manager. His own research into the history of individual objects has been particularly important in informing our chapters on sword, armor, and Ainu artifacts. All this was brought together under the inspired and untiring leadership of the Museum's Director of Public Programs, Richard Kissel.

We are also grateful to Maureen DaRos White and Rebekah DeAngelo, Catherine Sease, Eric Lazo-Wasem, Patrick Sweeney, and Kristof Zyskowski. Finally, we thank Peabody Director and Professor of Ecology David Skelly for his constant support.

Beyond the Museum, our curatorial consultants, Dani Botsman and Morgan Pitelka, made crucial contributions to the conceptual framing of the exhibition. Morihiro Ogawa's expertise was critical in allowing us to bring the collection of swords and armor to a wider public. Haruko Nakamura's great generosity with her time and knowledge allowed us to incorporate numerous rare books from the Sterling Memorial Library. At the Yale University Art Gallery, Sadako Ohki supported our loan requests and gave unstintingly of her expertise. Takuya Tsunoda negotiated permissions from Japanese institutions with tact and efficiency. Brandon Boyer, then in his junior year at Yale, informed the armor section with his energetic research. Hironori and Akiko Tsukamoto helped with translations. Adachi Sairei (Michiko) produced the Japanese calligraphy.

For their aid and advice, we are grateful to Adachi Tadashi, Marnie Anderson, Paola Bertucci, Aniko Bezur, Ron Bonanno, Michael Donoghue, Carol Forest, Ellen Hammond, Hasegawa Kazumi, Jordan Hamzawi, Hashimoto Mari, Hashimoto Ryōta, Robert Mormile, Erin Ross Myask, Hashizume Setsuya, Hirokawa Waka, Hitomi Tatsuo, Hitomi Akemi, Kawabata Chikako, Kathy Lu, Stacey Maples, Andrew Maske, Sara McDougall, Yasuo Ohdera, Okudaira Shunroku, Patricia Panico, Eric Rath, Nicholas Renouf, Jonathan Schlesinger, Timon Screech, Judith Ann Schiff and the Manuscripts and Archives staff at Sterling Memorial Library, Julie Stephens, Bill Sacco, David A. Sensabaugh, Tim Smith, Bernard Stoltie, Carrie Thiessen, Brian Turner, and Andrew Watsky. For the loan of objects, we are grateful to James Whitman; Susan Gibbons, Yale University Librarian; William Purvis, Director, Yale Collection of Musical Instruments; and Jock Reynolds, The Henry J. Heinz II Director, Yale University Art Gallery.

Finally, we are indebted to photographer William Guth, who volunteered his time and skill to capture many of the objects shown herein. This catalog would not have been possible without his talent and dedication.

The Authors

Catalog of the Exhibition

Numbered entries indicate materials from the exhibition that are shown in this catalog. Measurements are given in both metric and English units as height by width by depth, unless otherwise indicated.

Chapter 1
Samurai and the Culture of Japan's Great Peace

1 Samurai helmet and armor
Lacquered iron with silk lacing, and painted deer hides
(Late 18th to mid-19th century, in the style of the 13th to 14th century), documented repairs in 1855
Overall 167.6 × 76.2 × 73.7 cm (66 × 30 × 29 in.)
Maker unknown
Yale University Art Gallery, purchased with funds from the Japan Foundation Endowment of the Council on East Asian Studies, 2008.84.1a-r

Chapter 2
Before the Great Peace

Samurai bow
Black, white, and red fiber bindings
(Possibly 19th century)
Overall length 218.4 cm (86 in.)
YPM.ANT.056613
Donor, C. Arthur Ruickoldt (Yale 1907), 1942

2, 5 Six-panel folding screen (byōbu)
Scene from the Battle of Yashima from The Tale of the Heike
Ink, color, gold pigments, and flakes on paper
(Mid-17th century)
Unframed 95.1 × 282.6 cm (37.44 × 111.25 in.)
Artist unknown
Yale University Art Gallery, Leonard C. Hanna, Jr., Class of 1913, Fund, 2002.84.2

3 The Islands of Japan
Map © Fabian Drixler

4 Samurai blade (katana)
Steel
(15th century)
Signed, Yamato no kuni jūnin Kanesuke (大和國住人包助)
Length 88.3 cm (34.75 in.)
YPM.ANT.145432.001
Collector, Henry Walcott Farnam, 1953

5 See 2

6 "Samurai" crab
Paradorippe granulata (de Haan)
Carapace (body) width 20 mm (0.79 in.)
YPM.IZ.071593
Collector, E. S. Morse, 1876

7 The Sea Bed at Daimotsu Bay
Daimotsu no ura kaitei no zu
(1851)
Woodblock prints, triptych (reproduction)
Artist, Utagawa Kuniyoshi (1797–1861)
Overall 36.4 × 25.3 cm (14.3 × 10 in.)
Gift of Prof. Arthur R. Miller to the American Friends of the British Museum, © The Trustees of the British Museum, 2008,3037.20104

8 Lord Minamoto no Yoritomo's Hunt at the Foot of Mount Fuji
Minamoto no Yoritomo kō Fuji no susono makigari no zu, sanmai tsuzuki
(1810s)
Woodblock prints, triptych
Artist, Utagawa Kunisada (1786–1865)
Overall 38.1 × 77.5 cm (15 × 30.5 in.)
YPM.ANT.206753
Collector, Charles Schuchert, 1961; donor, Carl O. Dunbar, 1961

9a, 9b, 9c An Illustrated Biography of Oda Nobunaga
Ehon shūi Shinchōki, Vol. 1
(1803)
Woodblock prints
Author, Niwa Tōkei (1760–1822), with illustrations by Taga Jōkei (d. ca. 1810)
22.2 × 15.9 cm (8.75 × 6.25 in.); open 22.2 × 26.7 cm (8.75 × 10.5 in.)
On loan, courtesy Fabian Drixler

10 Kawabata Dōki brings the emperor his breakfast
Detail from Ie no kagami, a painted family history of Kawabata Dōki
Scroll, ink on paper (reproduction)
(Tokugawa period)
Private collection, courtesy of Kawabata Chikako

11 Samurai helmet and face mask
Steel and textile
(16th century)
Helmet length 40.6 cm (16 in.)
YPM.ANT.205043
Face mask length 25.4 cm (10 in.)
YPM.ANT.205044
Collector, Irene J. Morden, 1959

Chapter 3
The Art and Science of the Sword

12 Knife (kozuka) of a short sword (wakizashi) scabbard
Copper alloy
(Late 18th to early 19th century)
Overall length 21 cm (8.23 in.); handle length 9.5 cm (3.74 in.)
YPM.ANT.055519.002
Collector, John Sloane; donor, Evelyn Sloane Griswold, 1941

13 Short sword (wakizashi) blade
Steel
(17th to 18th century)
Signed, Hōshū-jū Fujiwara Masayuki (豊州住藤原正行)
Length 73.7 cm (29 in.)
YPM.ANT.055519.001
Collector, John Sloane; donor, Evelyn Sloane Griswold, 1941

14 Long sword (katana) blade
Steel
(15th century)
Unsigned
Length 99.1 cm (39 in.)
YPM.ANT.055520.001
Collector, John Sloane; donor, Evelyn Sloane Griswold, 1941

15 Long sword (katana) scabbard
Wood, lacquer, ray skin, copper alloy
(18th to 19th century)
Length 99.1 cm (39 in.)
YPM.ANT.055520.002
Collector, John Sloane; donor, Evelyn Sloane Griswold, 1941

16 Short sword (wakizashi) scabbard
Wood, lacquer, ray skin, copper alloy
(Late 18th to early 19th century)
Length 73.7 cm (29 in.)
YPM.ANT.055519.002
Collector, John Sloane; donor, Evelyn Sloane Griswold, 1941

17 Sword calamity amulet
Paper, ink
YPM.ANT.013383.003
Donor, John K. Hyde DeForest, 1881

18 Short sword (wazkiashi) blade
Steel
(Mid-19th century)
Signed, Ōshū-jū Nagamichi (奥州住長道), dated 1861

Length 55.9 cm (22 in.)
YPM.ANT.143394.001
Collector and donor, Shepherd
Stevens, 1949

19 Long sword (*katana*) blade
Steel
(16th century)
Signed, Bishū Osafune
Sukesada (備州長舩祐定)
Length 86.4 cm (34 in.)
YPM.ANT.143393.001
Collector and donor, Shepherd
Stevens, 1949

**20 Short sword
(*wakizashi*) scabbard**
Wood, lacquer, ray skin,
copper alloy
(19th century)
Length 99.1 cm (24 in.)
YPM.ANT.143394.002
Collector and donor, Shepherd
Stevens, 1949

21 Long sword (*katana*) scabbard
Wood, lacquer, ray skin,
copper alloy, gold
(Late 18th to early 19th century)
Length 93.9 cm (37 in.)
YPM.ANT.143393.002
Collector and donor, Shepherd
Stevens, 1949

**22 *The Swordsmith of Mount Inari
Inari-yama kokaji***
(1887)
From *Gekkō's Miscellany
Gekkō zuihitsu*
(1886–1887)
Woodblock print
Artist, Ogata Gekkō (1859–1920)
36.8 × 24.8 cm (14.5 × 9.75 in.)
YPM.ANT.144956
Donor, The Estate of Jeannette
M. K. Griswold, 1951

**23 Short sword (*wakizashi*)
blade restoration**
Inscribed, Ōshū-jū Nagamichi
(奥州住長道), dated 1861
YPM.ANT.143394.001
Photographers, Okisato Fujishiro
(藤代興里) and Akiko Myōga
(と冥賀明子). Courtesy of Okisato Fujishiro.

*The Museum gratefully acknowledges
the E. Rhodes and Leona B. Carpenter
Foundation for its support of this restoration.*

*Chapter 4
Edo and the Architecture
of the Great Peace*

**24, 27, 120 Lacquer
food bowl (*jikirō*)**
(Possibly early 17th century)
Lacquer, pitch, resin
26.7 cm (10.5 in.);
max. diam. 36.8 cm (14.5 in.)
YPM.ANT.241835
Collector, Mabel Loomis Todd, 1896;
donor, Millicent Todd Bingham, 1964

25 *Daimyo Territories in 1664*
© Fabian Drixler

**26 *Japan's Great Peace in
Global Context, 1550–1875***
© Fabian Drixler

27 See 24

28a–h, 29a–d Folding screens
A panorama of Edo (reproduction)
Edo-zu byōbu
(Likely painted between
1654 and 1662)
164.5 × 364.5 cm (64.75 × 143.5 in.)
Courtesy of the National Museum
of Japanese History

Yui (station 17)
YPM.ANT.144950
Mitsuke (station 29)
YPM.ANT.144935
Yokkaichi (station 44)
YPM.ANT.144941
From the series *Fifty-Three
Stations of the Tōkaidō
Tōkaidō gojūsan tsugi no uchi*
(1833–1834, later printing)
Woodblock prints
Artist, Utagawa Hiroshige
(1797–1858)
Each, 24 × 35 cm (9.25 × 13.75 in.)
Donor, The Estate of Jeannette
M. K. Griswold, 1951

**30 *Evening Rain at Koizumi
Koizumi no yau***
From the series *Eight Views
of Kanazawa
Kanazawa hakkei*
(ca. 1835–1836, later printing)
Woodblock print
Artist, Utagawa Hiroshige
(1797–1858)
24 × 35 cm (9.25 × 13.75 in.)
YPM.ANT.144949
Donor, The Estate of Jeannette
M. K. Griswold, 1951

*Sudden Rain at Tadasugawara
Tadasugawara no yūdachi*
From the series Famous
Sights of Kyoto
Kyōto meisho no uchi
(ca. 1834, later printing)
Woodblock print
Artist, Utagawa Hiroshige
(1797–1858)
24 × 35 cm (9.25 × 13.75 in.)
YPM.ANT.144952
Donor, The Estate of Jeannette
M. K. Griswold, 1951

31 A daimyo procession
Scroll, ink on paper (reproduction)
(Undated)
Artist, unknown
Tokyo National Museum Image Archives

32 Raincoat
Hemp palm
(19th century)
96.5 × 106.7 × 22.9 cm (38 × 42 × 9 in.)
YPM.ANT.236949

Collector, Mabel Loomis Todd, 1896;
donor, Millicent Todd Bingham, 1964

33 Sandals
Straw
(19th century)
14.6 × 25.4 × 10.2 cm (4 × 10 × 5.75 in.)
YPM.ANT.206468
Collector, Norvin J. Hein, 1960

*Chapter 5
Armament or Ornament?*

34, 36 Samurai helmet
Steel, lacquer, silk
(17th to 19th century; helmet
bowl probably 16th century)
Signed, Hosokawa, Daimyo
of Kumamoto
Helmet bowl 14 × 31 × 25 cm
(5.5 × 12.2 × 9.8 in.)
YPM.ANT.205042.001
Collector, Irene J. Morden, 1959

35 Samurai sleeves
Silk, ivory, copper alloy
(17th to 19th century)
67 × 20 cm (26.4 × 7.9 in.)
YPM.ANT.205042
Collector, Irene J. Morden, 1959

36 See 34

37 Samurai face mask
Steel, lacquer, silk
(17th to 19th century)
22 × 21 × 17 cm (8.7 × 8.3 × 6.7 in.)
YPM.ANT.205042
Collector, Irene J. Morden, 1959

Armor storage boxes
Wood, leather, iron or steel
(17th to 19th century)
61 × 43.2 × 43.2 cm (24 × 17 × 17 in.)
YPM.ANT.205042.002
Collector, Irene J. Morden, 1959

*Essentials for Knights
Tanki yōryaku*
(1729)
Woodblock prints (reproduction)
Author, Murai Masahiro (active
1729–1754)
26 cm (10.25 in.)
Sterling Memorial Library, Yale University,
EAL J1797

38 Samurai helmet and armor
Steel, lacquer, silk
(18th century)
94 × 61 × 29.2 cm (37 × 24 × 11 in.)
YPM.ANT.206517
Collector, Norvin J. Hein, 1960

39 Samurai helmet and armor
Steel, lacquer, silk
(17th to 19th century)
170.2 × 53.3 × 33 cm (67 × 21 × 13 in.)
YPM.ANT.243224.001
Collector, E. Stanley Pratt, 1973

40 Samurai helmet and armor
(17th to 19th century)
Steel, lacquer, silk, leather

Helmet and mask 40.6 × 40.6 × 35.6 cm
(16 × 16 × 14 in.)
YPM.ANT.013329
Donor, Othniel C. Marsh, 1889
Photograph © 2004 Harold
Shapiro, used with permission.

41   Stirrups
Steel, silver, lacquer, cinnabar
(18th century)
Signed, Kunitsugu, resident
  of Kaga province
22.9 × 27.9 × 14 cm (9 × 11 × 5.5 in.)
YPM.ANT.013329.010
Donor, Othniel C. Marsh, 1889

Armor storage box
Wood, steel
(17th to 19th century)
53 × 43 × 43 cm (20.9 × 16.9 × 16.9 in.)
YPM.ANT.013329.012
Donor, Othniel C. Marsh, 1889

Samurai helmet and face mask
Steel, lacquer, silk, leather
(18th century)
Overall 43.2 × 33 × 30.5 cm
(17 × 13 × 12 in.)
YPM.ANT.144450.002
Donor, John S. Moore, 1951

Signaling baton (*saihai*) and fan
Bamboo, wood, paper, metal
(Possibly 19th century)
Baton, 36.5 × 15.2 × 15.2 cm
(14.38 × 6 × 6 in.)
Fan, 29.2 × 39.8 × 1.9 cm
(11.5 × 15.5 × 0.75 in.)
YPM.ANT.205045
Collector, Irene J. Morden, 1959

42   *The Magistrate of Hakodate*
   with Two Attendants
Lithograph (reproduction)
(1854)
Artist, Wilhelm Heine (1827–1888)
Published in M.C. Perry and Francis L. Haws,
Narrative of the Expedition of an American
Squadron to the China Seas and Japan,
Vol.1, Washington, D.C.: Beverley Tucker,
1856
Private collection, courtesy of Fabian Drixler

Chapter 6
Samurai Aesthetics:
Extravagance and Restraint

43, 44   Box for writing implements
Hiramaki-e and *takamaki-e*
  with gold alloys and silver
(18th century)
Unsigned
5.1 × 26 × 22.9 cm (2 × 10.25 × 9 in.)
YPM.ANT.020548
Collector, Elizabeth Lauder Kellum, 1932

45   Lacquer tray with animal
   figures and eclipse
Takamaki-e
(Early 18th century)
Unsigned
3.2 × 27.3 × 21.6 cm
(1.25 × 10.75 × 8.5 in.)
YPM. ANT.057197
Anonymous gift, 1940

46   *The Popular Type*
Hayarisō
From the series
  32 Modern-Day Types
Tōsei sanjūni sō
(ca. 1822–1823)
Woodblock print
Artist, Utagawa Kunisada
  (1786–1865)
38.1 × 25.4 cm (15 × 10 in.)
YPM.ANT.144957
Donor, The Estate of Jeannette
M. K. Griswold, 1951

47   Bronze mirror with
   lacquer container
Hiramaki-e
(Late 18th century)
39.1 × 27 × 4.1 cm
(15.38 × 10.63 × 1.63 in.)
YPM.ANT.202834
Collector, Helen Wells Seymour, 1957

48   Small box
Togidashi and *takamaki-e* with
  gold and silver pattern
(16th century)
Unsigned
6 × 11.4 × 8.9 cm (2.38 × 4.5 × 3.5 in.)
YPM. ANT.020528
Collector, Elizabeth Lauder Kellum, 1932

49   Stationery box
Kamakura-bori style
(18th century)
Unsigned
23.2 × 18.7 × 4.8 cm
(9.13 × 7.38 × 1.88 in.)
YPM.ANT.057177
Anonymous gift, 1940

50   Presentation box
   featuring spiny lobsters
Takamaki-e with gold and cinnabar
(Mid-19th century)
Signed, [Yamada] Jōkasai
  (1811–1879)
10.9 × 23.2 × 8.9 cm
(4.13 × 9.13 × 3.5 in.)
YPM.ANT.231910
Collector, Thomas Sedgwick Van
Volkenburgh (YC 1866);
The Florence Baiz Van Volkenburgh
Gift in memory of her husband Thomas
Sedgwick Van Volkenburgh, 1968

51   Vanity box with
   articles and mirror
Hiramaki-e
(19th century)
Unsigned
10.2 × 17.8 cm (4 × 7 in.)
YPM.ANT.231909
Collector, Thomas Sedgwick Van
Volkenburgh (YC 1866);
The Florence Baiz Van Volkenburgh
Gift in memory of her husband Thomas
Sedgwick Van Volkenburgh, 1968

Inrō featuring sword motif
Five compartments, red lacquer,
  gold, mother of pearl
(18th century)
Signed, Kajikawa Family

10.2 × 5.1 × 3.3 cm (4 × 2 × 1.25 in.);
fob 3.8 × 3.8 × 2.2 cm
(1.5 × 1.5 × 0.88 in.)
YPM.ANT.231937
Collector, Thomas Sedgwick Van
Volkenburgh (YC 1866);
The Florence Baiz Van Volkenburgh
Gift in memory of her husband Thomas
Sedgwick Van Volkenburgh, 1968

52   *Inrō* depicting a kite
   tethered to a tree
Five compartments, black lacquer,
  ivory *netsuke* and silver *ojime*
(17th century)
Signed, Kajikawa Family
10.2 × 5.1 × 3.3 cm (4 × 2 × 1.25 in.);
netsuke 3.8 × 3.8 × 3.2 cm
(1.5 × 1.5 × 1.25 in.)
YPM.ANT.231940
Collector, Thomas Sedgwick
Van Volkenburgh (YC 1866); The
Florence Baiz Van Volkenburgh Gift
in memory of her husband Thomas
Sedgwick Van Volkenburgh, 1968

53   *Inrō* with wooden *netsuke*
   of a monk and carnelian *ojime*
(18th century)
Unsigned
9.5 × 5 × 3.2 cm (3.75 × 2 × 1.25 in.);
netsuke 6.4 × 2.2 × 1.9 cm
(2.5 × 0.9 × 0.75 in.)
YPM.ANT.231939
Collector, Thomas Sedgwick Van
Volkenburgh (YC 1866);
The Florence Baiz Van Volkenburgh
Gift in memory of her husband Thomas
Sedgwick Van Volkenburgh, 1968

54   Hanging scroll
Ink on paper
(1717)
Artist, Tsurusawa Tanzan
  (1655–1729)
188 × 50.8 cm (74 × 20 in.)
YPM.ANT.013425
Collector, A. J. Smith, 1906

Tea bowl
Ceramic
(17th to 18th century)
Likely Karatsu kiln
Diam. 12.7 cm (5 in.)
YPM.ANT.201907
Collector, Helen Wells Seymour, 1957

55   Tea caddy and bag
Ceramic, cloth, ivory
(18th to 19th century)
Caddy 9.84 × 6.03 × 4.45 cm
(3.88 × 2.38 × 1.75 in.);
bag 11.43 × 5.4 × 5.4 cm
(4.5 × 2.13 × 2.13 in.)
YPM.ANT.201949
Collector, Helen Wells Seymour, 1957

56   Flower vase
Ceramic
(19th to 20th century)
Possibly Takatori kiln
Height 48.3 cm (19 in.)
YPM.ANT.201987
Collector, Helen Wells Seymour, 1957

57 Stoneware water jar
with black lacquer lid
Ceramic, wood, lacquer
(19th to 20th century)
Artisan, Asami Gorōsuke
Height 15.2 cm (6 in.)
YPM.ANT.201965
Collector, Helen Wells Seymour, 1957

58 *Ryūteki* flute
Lacquered bamboo
(Late 19th century)
Overall length 42.6 cm (16.8 in.)
Yale Collection of Musical Instruments,
Anonymous gift, 3292.1950

59 *Shōjō* mask
Wood with red finish
(Likely 17th century)
Height 21 cm (8.25 in.)
YPM.ANT.206471
Collector, Norvin J. Hein, 1960

60 Shoulder drum
(*kotsuzumi*) core
Wood, lacquer
(Early 19th century)
25.1 × 9.8 × 9.8 cm
(9.9 × 3.9 × 3.9 in.)
YPM.ANT.057194
Anonymous gift, 1940

61 Hip drum (*ōtsuzumi*)
Wood, lacquer, silk, leather
(Likely early 18th century)
29.2 × 22.5 × 22.5 cm
(11.5 × 8.9 × 8.9 in.)
YPM.ANT.145685
Collector, A. J. Smith, 1906

62 Noh robe
Compounded twill, brocaded silk
(Late 18th century)
Length in back 146.7 cm (57.75 in.);
overall width 140 cm (55.1 in.)
Yale University Art Gallery, Hobart
and Edward Small Moore Memorial
Collection, Bequest of Mrs. William
H. Moore, 1955.39.1

63 Noh robe
Compound twill brocade with
silk and metallic thread
(Likely 18th century)
Overall 159 × 131.5 cm (62.6 × 51.75 in.)
Yale University Art Gallery, Gift of
Mrs. Jared K. Morse, 1952.40.26

Chapter 7
The Samurai Imagined

64, 70a, 70b *Illustrated
Encyclopedia of the Theater
Shibai kinmōzui*
(1803, Meiji-era printing)
Woodblock-printed book,
8 volumes bound as 1
Author, Shikitei Sanba (1776–1822),
with illustrations by Katsukawa
Shun'ei (1762–1819) and
Utagawa Toyokuni I (1769–1825)
22.5 × 16 cm (8.9 × 6.3 in.)
Sterling Memorial Library, Yale University,
EAL J0495

65 *Chūshingura, Act XI:
The Night Raid
Chūshingura jūichidanme
yo-uchi no zu*
(ca. 1831)
Oban, polychrome woodblock print
(reproduction)
Artist, Utagawa Kuniyoshi
(1797–1861)
25 × 37 cm (9.8 × 14.6 in.)
Yale University Art Gallery, Gift of Mr. and
Mrs. J. Watson Webb B.A. 1907, 1942.71

66a, 66b *An Illustrated
Chūshingura
Ehon Chūshingura*
(1800)
Woodblock-printed book, 4 volumes
of 10 (20 including sequel
volumes published in 1808)
Author and illustrator, Hayami
Shungyōsai (1767–1823)
22 × 15.5 cm (8.7 × 6.1 in.)
Sterling Memorial Library, Yale University,
EAL J0054

67a, 67b, 67c *The Iroha Library
Iroha bunko*
(1836–1872)
Woodblock-printed book,
54 volumes
Author, Vols. 1–12, Tamenaga
Shunsui I (1790–1844), with
illustrations by Keisai Eisen
(1790–1848) and others;
remaining volumes by
Tamenaga Shunsui II (1818–
1886) and various artists
17.5 × 12 cm (6.9 × 4.7 in.)
Sterling Memorial Library, Yale University,
EAL J0906, EAL J0907

68 *A View of the Flourishing
of Kabuki in Edo
Odori keiyō Edo-e no sakae*
(1858)
Woodblock prints, triptych
(reproduction)
Artist, Utagawa Toyokuni III
(Utagawa Kunisada) (1786–1864)
Each 37 × 25 cm (14.6 × 9.8 in.)
Courtesy of the Tsubouchi Memorial Theatre
Museum, Waseda University, Tokyo,
118-0087, 118-0088, 118-0089

69 *The Prosperity of
the Eastern Capital
Tōto han'ei no zu*
(1854)
Woodblock prints, triptych, from
a set of 9 prints (reproduction)
Artist, Utagawa Hiroshige
(1797–1858)
Each 36 × 24.5–25.5 cm
(14.2 × 9.6–10 in.)
National Diet Library, Tokyo,
01-001, 01-002, 01-003

*Perspective Print Depicting
a Kabuki Performance
Shibai kyōgen ukie*
(ca. 1763)
Woodblock print (reproduction)
Artist, Torii Kiyotsune (dates unknown;
flourished ca. 1750–1780)

31 × 45 cm (12.2 × 17.7 in.)
Courtesy of the Tsubouchi Memorial
Theatre Museum, Waseda
University, Tokyo, 118-0083

70 See 64

71 *Shamisen*
(19th century)
Overall length 97.3 cm (38.3 in.)
Yale Collection of Musical Instruments,
Anonymous Gift, 4402.1972

72 *Thirty-Six Flowers of the Stage
Yakusha Sanjūrokkasen*
(1835)
Woodblock-printed book, 1 volume
Authors, Utagawa Kunisada
(Utagawa Toyokuni III) (1786–
1864) and Totoya Hokkei
(1780–1850), with preface by
Ryūtei Tanehiko (1783–1842)
25.5 × 18.5 cm (10 × 7.3 in.)
Sterling Memorial Library, Yale University,
EAL J0028

*Sights of the Eastern Capital:
The Prosperity of the Theater
District
Tōto meisho shibai-chō
han'ei no zu*
(ca. 1840)
Woodblock print (reproduction)
Artist, Utagawa Hiroshige I
(1797–1858)
23.5 × 35.5 cm (9.25 × 14 in.)
Courtesy of the Tsubouchi Memorial Theatre
Museum, Waseda University, Tokyo,
118-0199

73 Woodblock for a fan print
of *The Five Men: Kaminari
("Thunder") Shōkurō
Gonin otoko no uchi:
Kaminari Shōkurō*
(ca. 1850)
Artist, Utagawa Toyokuni III
(Utagawa Kunisada)
24.5 × 33.7 × 1.9 cm
(9.6 × 13.25 × 0.75 in.)
YPM.ANT.202096
Collector, Helen Wells Seymour, 1957

74 *The Five Men: Kaminari
("Thunder") Shōkurō
Gonin otoko no uchi:
Kaminari Shōkurō*
(ca. 1850)
Recreation of woodblock print,
by William D. Fleming and Sally Pallatto
© Yale Peabody Museum of Natural History

75a, 75b, 75c *The Actors'
Romance of the Three Kingdoms
Yakusha fūzoku sangokushi*
(1831)
Woodblock-printed book,
3 volumes
Author, Hanagasa Bunkyō
(1785–1860), with illustrations
by Ryūsai Shigeharu
(1802–1852)
22.5 × 15.5 cm (8.9 × 6.1 in.)
Sterling Memorial Library, Yale University,
EAL J0856

76 A Humorous Collection of
  Jewels of the Floating World
Dōke ukiyo tama-zukushi
(1864)
Woodblock prints, triptych
Artist, Utagawa Yoshitora
  (dates unknown)
38.1 × 73.7 cm (15 × 29 in.)
YPM.ANT.206760
Collector, Charles Schuchert, 1961;
donor, Carl O. Dunbar, 1961

Chapter 8
Death and the Good Life

77, 87a–o A Mirror of
  People's Hearts
Banmin kokoro no kagami
(1854)
Author, Ishida Ryūgen (1821–1875),
  with illustrations by Ōsuka
  Kiyomitsu (d. 1875)
26 cm (10.25 in.)
Sterling Memorial Library, Yale University,
EAL J1730

Buddha with halo
Wood, paint
Overall 47 × 17.8 × 16.5 cm
(18.5 × 7 × 6.5 in.)
YPM.ANT.206514
Collector, Norvin J. Hein, 1960

Shrine
Wood, paint
Closed 10.2 × 4.1 × 2.5 cm
(4 × 1.6 × 1 in.)
YPM.ANT.057206
Anonymous gift, 1940

Shrine
Wood, paint
Open 14 × 12.7 × 5.7 cm
(5.5 × 5 × 2.25 in.)
YPM.ANT.206489
Collector, Norvin J. Hein, 1960

Buddha with box
Wood, paint
31.7 × 27.3 × 19.7 cm
(12.5 × 10.8 × 7.8 in.)
YPM.ANT.205037
Collector, Irene J. Morden, 1959

78 The bodhisattva
  Kannon of eleven faces
  and a thousand hands
Wood, paint
(1692, inscribed)
35.6 × 21.6 × 15.2 cm
(14 × 8.5 × 6 in.)
YPM.ANT.013377
Donor, John K. Hyde DeForest, 1881

Shrine with statuary
Wood, paint
Open 40.6 × 50.2 × 25.4 cm
(16 × 19.75 × 10 in.)
YPM.ANT.013376
Donor, John K. Hyde DeForest, 1881

Gold shrine
Wood, paint
21.6 × 8.3 × 4.8 cm (8.5 × 3.25 × 1.9 in.)

YPM.ANT.013386
Donor, John K. Hyde DeForest, 1881

Memorial tablet
Wood, paint
43.2 × 16.8 × 8.3 cm (6.6 × 17 × 3.25 in.)
YPM.ANT.013332
Donor, John K. Hyde DeForest, 1881

79 Memorial tablet
Wood, paint
41.9 × 16.5 × 8.3 cm
(16.5 × 6.5 × 3.25 in.)
YPM.ANT.013331
Donor, John K. Hyde DeForest, 1881

80 Memorial tablet
Wood, paint
43.8 × 15.9 × 7.9 cm
(6.25 × 17.25 × 3.1 in.)
YPM.ANT.013333
Donor, John K. Hyde DeForest, 1881

Memorial tablet
Wood, paint
40 × 16.5 × 14 cm (15.75 × 6.5 × 5.5 in.)
YPM.ANT.013330
Donor, John K. Hyde DeForest, 1881

Shrine
Wood, paint, metal
20.3 × 10.2 × 10.2 cm (8 × 4 × 4 in.);
open 14 cm (5.5 in.)
YPM.ANT.013388
Donor, John K. Hyde DeForest, 1881

81, 82 Folding screens (*byōbu*)
Scenes from *The 24*
  Paragons of Filial Piety
(Late 17th to early 19th century)
Signed, Masanobu
119.4 × 251.5 cm (47 × 99 in.)
On loan, courtesy James Whitman

83 A Guide to the Prosperity
  of Future Generations
Shison hanjō tebikigusa
(Undated edition, but similar in
  style to dated editions from
  between 1826 and 1857)
Woodblock-printed book
Author, Anonymous
22.9 × 15.9 cm (9 × 6.25 in.)
On loan, courtesy Fabian Drixler

84 Personal copybook with a
  handwritten copy of *Manual*
  for Ensuring the Prosperity
  of Future Generations
Shison hanjō tebikigusa
(ca. 1835, a date that appears
  in another part of the book)
Author, unknown
25 cm (9.8 in.)
Sterling Memorial Library, Yale University,
EAL J1724

85 Avoid Evil and Do Good!
  Japanese Verses on Extending
  Life and Rearing Children
Shoaku bakusaku, shozen bugyō
  enmei kosodate wasan
(Probably early to mid-19th century)
Woodblock-printed book

Author, Giten from Usui
  district in Kōzuke
16 cm (6.3 in.)
Sterling Memorial Library, Yale University,
EAL J1762

86 On Children Born in
  a Fire-Horse Year
Hinoeuma umareko no oshiegaki
(Undated, but known to be 1845)
Woodblock print
Author, Komazuka Senkai of
  Izumi province; artist, Hōrai
  Shunshō (Utagawa Kunimori,
  flourished ca. 1845)
37.2 × 25.4 cm (14.6 × 10 in.)
On loan, courtesy Fabian Drixler

87 See *77*

88 Amulet bundle
Paper, ink
YPM.ANT.013383.002,
YPM.ANT.013383.003
Donor, John K. Hyde DeForest, 1881

89 An amulet for safe
  childbirth (*Anzan-mamori*)
Paper, ink
7.9 × 2.5 cm (3.1 × 1 in.)
YPM.ANT.013367.002
Donor, John K. Hyde DeForest, 1881

Magic spell amulet
Paper, ink
10.2 × 8.9 cm (3.5 × 4 in.)
YPM.ANT.013367.003
Donor, John K. Hyde DeForest, 1881

90 Fukurokuju, a Daoist Immortal
  and God of Good Fortune
Wood, walrus ivory, mother of pearl
7.9 × 5.1 × 2.9 cm
(3.13 × 2 × 1.1 in.)
YPM.ANT.231941
Collector, Thomas Sedgwick Van
Volkenburgh (YC 1866);
The Florence Baiz Van Volkenburgh
Gift in memory of her husband Thomas
Sedgwick Van Volkenburgh, 1968

91 A Realm at Peace
Tenga taihei
(Likely early 19th century)
Woodblock print
Artist unknown
38.1 × 25.4 cm (15 × 10 in.)
YPM.ANT.144966
Donor, The Estate of Jeannette
M. K. Griswold, 1951

Chapter 9
Forbidden Waters
and Foreign Knowledge

92, 97 A New Book
  of Eye Medicine
Ganka shinsho
(1812–1813)
Hand-colored woodblock print
Author, Sugita Ryūkei (1786–1845),
  translated from Joseph Jacob
  Plenck, with illustrations by
  Ishikawa Tairō (1765–1817)

25 × 17.5 cm (9.75 × 6.1 in.)
On loan, courtesy William D. Fleming

**93 The Great Martyrdom
of Nagasaki
Martirio dei 70 Giapponesi
ed Europei a Nagasaki**
(1626–1632)
Painting (reproduction)
Anonymous Japanese artist,
painted in Macao
Courtesy of the Chiesa del Gesù in Rome;
photograph © 2006 Zeno Colantoni

**94 A cross of the
hidden Christians**
Metal
2.5 × 20 cm (7.9 × 9.9 in.)
On loan, courtesy Fabian Drixler

**95 Register of religious
surveillance**
*Kirishitan sensaku shūmon
aratamechō*
(Kamijōarai village, 1666)
Woodblock-printed book
34 cm (13.4 in.)
Sterling Memorial Library, Yale University,
EAL J1732

**96 Illustrations of Strange
Diseases and Their
Surgical Treatments**
Kishitsu geryō zukan
(Undated hand copy)
Hand-colored woodblock print
(reproduction)
Author, Hanaoka Seishū
(1760–1835)
28 cm (11 in.)
U.S. National Library of Medicine,
National Institutes of Health, 101147736

97 See 92

98 Various Tales from the Dutch
Kōmō zatsuwa
(1787)
Woodblock-printed book
Author, Morishima Chūryō
(1756–1810)
23 × 16 cm (6.25 × 9 in.)
Sterling Memorial Library, Yale University,
EAL J0894

**99a, 99b A Foreign-Themed
Parody of Chūshingura**
Karadehon Tōjingura
(1796)
Woodblock-printed book
(reproduction)
Author, most likely Morishima
Chūryō (1756–1810), most
likely illustrated by Kitao
Shigemasa (1739–1820)
18 × 12.5 cm (7.1 × 4.9 in.)
Waseda University Library,
13 01961 0151

**Aerial View of the Harbor at
Nagasaki with the Dutch Frigate
Cornelia and Henriette**
Panel, gouache, silk (reproduction)
(ca. 1840)

Artist, Kawahara Keiga
(1786–after 1860)
57.2 × 80 × 0.2 cm
(22.5 × 31.5 × 0.06 in.)
Peabody Essex Museum, M20148

*Chapter 10
Japan in Ainu Lands*

**100 Lacquer cup or bowl
(tuki) with pedestal**
Wood, lacquer
5.7 × 14 × 14.3 cm (2.25 × 5.5
× 5.6 in.); pedestal 14 × 14 ×
6 cm (5.5 × 5.5 × 2.4 in.)
YPM.ANT.140594
Collector, Frank Benedict Cleland, 1947

101 Necklace
Glass, metal
28.6 × 36.2 × 3.2 cm
(11.25 × 14.25 × 1.25 in.)
YPM.ANT.209149
Collector, Mabel Loomis Todd, 1896;
donor, Millicent Todd Bingham, 1964

102 Attush robe
Treebark fibers with indigo-
dyed Japanese cloth
118 × 127 cm (46.5 × 50 in.)
YPM.ANT.209411
Collector, G. Nakajima, 1965;
Yale Peabody Museum purchase

**103a–c, 116a–b, 118a–b
Curious Sights of
the Isles of Ezo**
Ezo-tō kikan
(1799)
Hand-colored woodblock
prints (reproductions)
Author, Murakami Shimanojō
Courtesy of the National Museum in Tokyo

104 Ruunpe robe
Imported Japanese fabrics
124.5 × 127 cm (49 × 50 in.)
YPM.ANT.209413
Collector, G. Nakajima, 1965;
Yale Peabody Museum purchase

105 Attush robe
Treebark fibers with indigo-
dyed Japanese cloth
120 × 125 cm (47.25 × 49.25 in.)
YPM.ANT.209407
Collector, G. Nakajima, 1965;
Yale Peabody Museum purchase

**106 Multi-purpose
carving knife (makiri)**
Wood, metal, bone
33 × 7.9 × 2.7 cm
(13 × 3.13 × 1.13 in.)
YPM.ANT.140607
Collector, Frank Benedict Cleland, 1947

**107 Multi-purpose
carving knife (makiri)**
Wood, steel, bone, plant fiber
Overall length 30.5 cm (12 in.)
YPM.ANT.206391
Donor, Norvin J. Hein, 1960

**108 Multi-purpose
carving knife (makiri)**
Wood, steel, plant fiber
(19th century)
Overall length 31 cm (12.2 in.)
YPM.ANT.209148
Collector, Mabel Loomis Todd, 1896;
donor, Millicent Todd Bingham, 1964

**109 Multi-purpose
carving knife (makiri)**
Wood, metal
26 × 5.7 × 2.3 cm
(10.25 × 2.25 × 0.9 in.)
YPM.ANT.209147
Collector, Mabel Loomis Todd, 1896;
donor, Millicent Todd Bingham, 1964

**110 Smoking kit (tanpakuop),
consisting of a pipe holder
and a tobacco box**
Wood, bone, plant fibers
Box 7.9 × 9.5 × 4.8 cm
(3.1 × 3.75 × 1.9 in.); rack 30.3 × 3.2
× 0.95 cm (12 × 1.25 × 0.4 in.)
YPM.ANT.140610
Collector, Frank Benedict Cleland, 1947

**Smoking kit (tanpakuop),
consisting of a pipe holder
and a tobacco box**
Wood, bone, plant fibers
Box 7 × 9.5 × 4.5 cm (2.75 ×
3.75 × 1.75 in.); rack 20.3 × 2.7
× 1.9 cm (8 × 1.1 × 0.75 in.)
YPM.ANT.140611
Collector, Frank Benedict Cleland, 1947

111 Pipe
Wood, stone
22.9 × 3.2 × 1.9 cm (9 × 1.25 × 0.75 in.)
YPM.ANT.209146
Collector, Mabel Loomis Todd, 1896;
donor, Millicent Todd Bingham, 1964

Pipes
Wood
Diam. 1.9 cm (0.5 in.); overall
lengths 25.4 cm (10 in.), 18.4 cm
(7.25 in.), 16.5 cm (6.5 in.)
YPM.ANT.206395
Collector, Norvin J. Hein, 1960

Ikupasuy
Wood
32.7 × 4.8 × 1.6 cm (12.9 × 1.9 × 0.6 in.)
YPM.ANT.209641
Collector, G. Nakajima, 1966;
Yale Peabody Museum purchase

112 Ikupasuy
Wood, lacquer
34 × 2.2 × 3.2 cm (13.4 × 0.9 × 0.1 in.)
YPM.ANT.209144
Collector, Mabel Loomis Todd, 1896;
donor, Millicent Todd Bingham, 1964

113 Ikupasuy
Wood, lacquer
32.4 × 3.2 × 0.6 cm (12.75
× 1.25 × 0.25 in.)
YPM.ANT.209643
Collector, G. Nakajima, 1966;
Yale Peabody Museum purchase

114 Ikupasuy
Wood, lacquer
35.6 × 3.2 × 0.6 cm
(14 × 1.25 × 0.25 in.)
YPM.ANT.140613
Collector, Frank Benedict Cleland, 1947

Ikupasuy
Wood
30.8 × 2.9 × 0.95 cm
(12.1 × 1.1 × 0.4 in.)
YPM.ANT.209649
Collector, G. Nakajima, 1966; Yale
Peabody Museum purchase

Ikupasuy
Wood
29.5 × 2.9 × 0.6 cm (11.6 × 1.1 × 0.25 in.)
YPM.ANT.209650
Collector, G. Nakajima, 1966;
Yale Peabody Museum purchase

Ikupasuy
Wood
36.5 × 29.9 × 1.9 cm
(14.4 × 1.75 × 0.75 in.)
YPM.ANT.209145
Collector, Mabel Loomis Todd, 1896;
donor, Millicent Todd Bingham, 1964

*115 Illustrated Overview
of Strange Lands
Ehon ikoku ichiran*
(1799)
Book (reproduction)
Author, Shunkōen Hanamaru and
Santō Kyōden (1761–1816),
illustrated by Okada Gyokuzan
(c. 1735–1808)
23 × 16 cm (9 × 6.3 in.)
Sterling Memorial Library, Yale University,
EAL J0125

116 See 103

*117 Stylized birds bearing
a prayer (inaw)*
Wood
33 × 12.7 × 1.9 cm (13 × 5 × 0.75 in.);
29.9 × 12.7 × 1.9 cm (11.75 × 5 × 0.75in.);
28.6 × 7.6 × 2.5 cm (11.25 × 3 × 1 in.)
YPM.ANT.206394
Collector, Norvin J. Hein, 1960

118 See 103

Bow
Wood
107.6 × 17.8 × 2.5 cm
(42.4 × 7 × 1 in.)
YPM.ANT.140599
Collector, Frank Benedict Cleland, 1947

Quiver with arrows
Wood, paint, plant fibers, feathers
60.1 × 13.3 × 6.4 cm (24 × 5.25 × 2.5 in.)
YPM.ANT.140600
Collector, Frank Benedict Cleland, 1947

Steller's sea eagle
Haliaeetus pelagicus (Pallas, 1811)
81.3 × 34.3 × 15.2 cm
(32 × 13.5 × 6 in.)
YPM.ORN.058634

Lacquer box
Wood, lacquer, paper, silk
45.7 × 38.1 × 38.1 cm (18 × 15 × 15 in.)
YPM.ANT.143389
Collector, Shepherd Stevens, 1949

Lacquer bowl
Wood, lacquer
17.5 × 33 × 27.9 cm (6.88 × 13 × 11 in.)
YPM.ANT.202842
Collector, Helen Wells Seymour, 1957

Lacquer tea caddy
Wood, lacquer
16.5 × 18.4 × 18.4 cm
(6.5 × 7.25 × 7.25 in.)
YPM.ANT.202021
Collector, Helen Wells Seymour, 1957

Wooden plate
Wood
1.9 × 18.4 × 18.4 cm
(0.75 × 7.25 × 7.25 in.)
YPM.ANT.209151
Collector, Mabel Loomis Todd, 1896;
donor, Millicent Todd Bingham, 1964

119 Lacquerware
Photographic print (reproduction)
(Unknown date)
Creator, unknown
Todd-Bingham Picture Collection,
1837–1966 (inclusive), Manuscripts &
Archives, Yale University Library, neg.
#A10-93, digital image no. 6862

120 See 24

121 Lacquer tea pot
Wood, lacquer
20.3 × 32.4 × 20 cm (8 × 12.75 × 7.9 in.)
YPM.ANT.209155
Collector, Mabel Loomis Todd, 1896;
donor, Millicent Todd Bingham, 1964

122 Round lacquer box
Wood, lacquer
11.8 × 10.5 × 10.5 cm
(4.63 × 4.13 × 4.13 in.)
YPM.ANT.209154
Collector, Mabel Loomis Todd, 1896;
donor, Millicent Todd Bingham, 1964

123 Shell game box
Wood, lacquer, metal
17.8 × 42.2 × 42.2 cm
(17 × 16.6 × 16.6 in.)
YPM.ANT.241837
Collector, Mabel Loomis Todd, 1896;
donor, Millicent Todd Bingham, 1964

Tray or dish
Wood
4.1 × 27.6 × 13.3 cm (1.6
× 10.9 × 5.25 in.)
YPM.ANT.209150
Collector, Mabel Loomis Todd, 1896;
donor, Millicent Todd Bingham, 1964

Tray or dish
Wood, lacquer
5.1 × 23.2 × 12.1 cm (2 × 9.1 × 4.75 in.)
YPM.ANT.209651
Collector, G. Nakajima, 1966; Yale
Peabody Museum purchase

Tray or dish
Wood
6.4 × 29.2 × 15.6 cm
(2.5 × 11.5 × 6.1 in.)
YPM.ANT.209652
Collector, G. Nakajima, 1966;
Yale Peabody Museum purchase

Necklace
Glass, plant fibers
25.7 × 19.1 × 2.9 cm (10.1 × 7.5 × 1.1 in.)
YPM.ANT.140597
Collector, Frank Benedict Cleland, 1947

Ikupasuy
Wood
35.2 × 2.9 × 0.95 cm
(13.9 × 1.1 × 0.4 in.)
YPM.ANT.209644
Collector, G. Nakajima, 1966;
Yale Peabody Museum purchase

Saké bottle gourd
Gourd, gold, shell inlay
24.1 × 9.5 × 9.5 cm
(9.5 × 3.75 × 3.75 in.)
YPM.ANT.057209
Anonymous gift, 1940

Sword with scabbard
Steel, wood, lacquer, silk, ray skin
(19th century)
Overall length 83 cm (32.7 in.)
YPM.ANT.010646
Donor, Tozaburo Kudo, 1906

Scabbard
Wood, lacquer, silk, ray
skin, shibichi alloy
Overall length 96.4 cm (36 in.)
YPM.ANT.145432
Collector, Henry Walcott Farnam, 1953

Sword
Steel, wood, lacquer, silk,
ray skin, copper alloy
(19th century)
Overall length 97.2 cm (38.25 in.)
YPM.ANT.145433
Collector, Henry Walcott Farnam, 1953

Sword
Steel, wood, lacquer, silk,
ray skin, copper alloy
(blade, 16th century;
scabbard, 19th century)
Overall length 99 cm (39 in.)
YPM.ANT.055518

Kodiak bear
Ursus arctos middendorffi Merriam,
1896
228.6 × 116.8 × 175.3 cm
(90 × 46 × 69 in.)
YPM.MAM.013686
Collector, R. H. Kopp, 1998

*Chapter 11
The Opening of Japan,
the Closing of the Great Peace*

124 Silk purse
Silk, copper alloy
(Late 19th century, Meiji period)

12.4 × 12.4 cm (4.9 × 4.9 in.);
extended 17.2 cm (6.75 in.)
YPM.ANT.202283
Collector, Helen Wells Seymour, 1957

125   *Daily Positions of
American Whaling Vessels*
© Fabian Drixler. From data assembled
between 2000 and 2010 during the
Census of Marine Life Project (www.coml.
org) by Tim D. Smith, Randall R. Reeves,
Elizabeth A. Josephson, and Judith N. Lund,
and made available for these maps.

126   Whale vertebra
54.6 × 78.1 × 29.2 cm
(21.5 × 30.75 × 11.5 in.)
YPM.MAM.013231

Whale lower jaw
Balaenopteridae
Each 101.6 × 17.8 × 14 cm
(40 × 7 × 5.5 in.)
YPM.MAM.013234,
YPM.MAM.013235

Sea otter skull
Enhydra lutris
7.3 × 17.2 × 10.8 cm
(2.9 × 6.75 × 4.25 in.)
YPM.MAM.007070

127   Tokugawa Yoshinobu
Photographic print (reproduction)
(1866 or 1867)
Creator, unknown
Tojō Museum of History, Matsudo City

128   Tokugawa Yoshinobu
Photographic print (reproduction)
(1866)
Creator, unknown
Ibaraki Prefectural Museum of History

Samurai sword scabbard ornament
(*menuki*), figurine, pin
Bronze, silver, gold
Overall length 4.1 cm (1.6 in.)
YPM.ANT.202184
Collector, Helen Wells Seymour, 1957

129   Samurai sword scabbard
ornament (*menuki*), seated man
Copper alloy
3.2 × 4.1 cm (1.25 × 1.6 in.)
YPM.ANT.202179
Collector, Helen Wells Seymour, 1957

130   Samurai sword scabbard
ornament (*menuki*), flowers, pin
Copper alloy, gold
1.6 × 4.5 cm (0.6 × 1.75 in.)
YPM.ANT.202185
Collector, Helen Wells Seymour, 1957

131   Samurai sword scabbard
ornament (*menuki*), fish
Copper alloy, gold
0.3 × 6.7 cm (0.1 × 2.6 in.)
YPM.ANT.202182
Collector, Helen Wells Seymour, 1957

Samurai sword scabbard ornament
(*menuki*), female figure
Copper alloy, gold

2.9 × 3.8 cm (1.1 × 1.5 in.)
YPM.ANT.202181
Collector, Helen Wells Seymour, 1957

Samurai sword scabbard
ornament (*menuki*), dragon, pin
Copper alloy
Overall length 6.4 cm (2.5 in.)
YPM.ANT.202183
Collector, Helen Wells Seymour, 1957

Samurai sword scabbard
ornament (*menuki*), male
figurine, animal, and drum, pin
Copper alloy, silver
Overall length 3.8 cm (1.5 in.)
YPM.ANT.202189
Collector, Helen Wells Seymour, 1957

Samurai sword scabbard ornament
(*menuki*), three fish, pin
Silver
35 × 1 cm (13.8 × 0.4 in.)
YPM.ANT.205274
Collector, Helen Wells Seymour, 1957

Samurai sword scabbard ornament
(*menuki*), samurai figure, pin
Copper alloy
1.6 × 3.8 cm (0.6 × 1.5 in.)
YPM.ANT.205271
Collector, Helen Wells Seymour, 1957

Samurai sword scabbard
ornament (*menuki*), insect, pin
Copper alloy
Overall length 4.1 cm (1.6 in.)
YPM.ANT.202190
Collector, Helen Wells Seymour, 1957

Samurai sword scabbard ornament
(*menuki*), male figurine, pin
Copper alloy
Overall length 3.8 cm (1.5 in.)
YPM.ANT.202187
Collector, Helen Wells Seymour, 1957

Samurai sword scabbard ornament
(*menuki*), two bats, pin
Silver
2.3 cm × 1.5 cm (0.9 × 0.6 in.)
YPM.ANT.205273
Collector, Helen Wells Seymour, 1957

132   Mabel Loomis Todd
Photographic print (reproduction)
(ca. 1907)
Creator, Elmer Chickering, Boston
Todd-Bingham Picture Collection, 1837–
1966 (inclusive). Manuscripts & Archives,
Yale University Library, digital image no. 205

133   Mabel Loomis Todd
Photographic print (reproduction)
(1896)
Creator, unknown
Todd-Bingham Picture Collection,
1837–1966 (inclusive). Manuscripts
& Archives, Yale University Library,
digital image no. 6859

134   Purse with button and
sword scabbard ornament
Leather, metal, ivory, shell
(Late 19th century, Meiji period)

8.6 × 15.2 cm (3.4 × 6 in.);
extended 22.2 cm (8.75 in.);
carved button diam. 4.5 cm (1.75 in.)
YPM.ANT.241869
Donor, Millicent Todd Bingham, 1964

135   *Inrō* with *netsuke* in
the shape of a theater
mask and ivory *ojime*
Black lacquer, gold, silver, ivory
(18th century)
Unsigned
10.2 × 5.1 × 3.8 cm
(4 × 2 × 1.5 in.);
netsuke 5.4 × 2.9 × 2.9 cm
(1.1 × 2.1 × 1.1 in.)
YPM.ANT.231936
Collector, Thomas Sedgwick Van
Volkenburgh (YC 1866);
The Florence Baiz Van Volkenburgh
Gift in memory of her husband Thomas
Sedgwick Van Volkenburgh, 1968

136   *Inrō* with ivory *netsuke*
and gold and silver *ojime*
Four compartments, lacquer, gold,
silver, mother of pearl, ivory
Unsigned
8.3 × 7 × 2.5 cm (3.25 × 2.75
× 1 in.); netsuke 4.5 × 2.2 × 2.2
cm (1.75 × 0.9 × 0.9 in.)
YPM. ANT.231935
Collector, Thomas Sedgwick Van
Volkenburgh (YC 1866);
The Florence Baiz Van Volkenburgh
Gift in memory of her husband Thomas
Sedgwick Van Volkenburgh, 1968

Inrō with netsuke decorated
with butterfly
Three compartments, black
lacquer, gold, silver, ivory
(18th century)
Unsigned
5.4 × 5.1 × 2.5 cm (2.1 × 2 × 1 in.);
fob 3.5 × 2.2 × 1.3 cm (1.4 × 0.9 × 0.5 in.)
YPM.ANT.231938
Collector, Thomas Sedgwick Van
Volkenburgh (YC 1866);
The Florence Baiz Van Volkenburgh
Gift in memory of her husband Thomas
Sedgwick Van Volkenburgh, 1968

137   Sword
Steel, wood, lacquer,
silver, ray skin, silk
(Late 19th century, Meiji period)
8.3 × 71.8 × 8.3 cm
(3.25 × 28.25 × 3.25 in.)
YPM.ANT.055516
Donor, Mrs. W. E. S. Griswold, 1941

138   Lacquer writing box
with implements and bag
(Late 19th century, Meiji period)
Wood, lacquer
3.8 × 14.6 × 16.5 cm (1.5 × 5.75 × 6.5 in.)
YPM.ANT.231908
Collector, Thomas Sedgwick Van
Volkenburgh (YC 1866);
The Florence Baiz Van Volkenburgh
Gift in memory of her husband Thomas
Sedgwick Van Volkenburgh, 1968

Sources
and Further Reading

Chapter 1
Samurai and the Culture
of Japan's Great Peace

Suga, Takaaki, "Perceptions of Edo-period Armor." *Bulletin of the Detroit Museum of Art,* vol. 88, no. 1/4 (2014).

Chapter 2
Before the Great Peace

Atwell, William S., "Climate Change, Mass Migration, and Political Upheaval in the Late Medieval Word." Paper presented at *Climate Change and Global Crisis in the Seventeenth Century,* KWI Essen, 6 May 2014.

Conlan, Thomas D., *State of War: The Violent Order of Fourteenth-Century Japan.* Ann Arbor: University of Michigan Center for Japanese Studies, 2003.

Farris, William Wayne, *Heavenly Warriors: The Evolution of Japan's Military, 500–1300.* Cambridge: Council on East Asian Studies, Harvard University, 1992.

Friday, Karl F., *Hired Swords: The Rise of Private Warrior Power in Early Japan.* Stanford: Stanford University Press, 1992.

Kamens, Edward, "*The Tale of Genji* and *Yashima* Screens in Local and Global Contexts." *Yale University Art Gallery Bulletin* (2007), p. 100–121.

Ikegami, Eiko, *The Taming of the Samurai: Honorific Individualism and the Making of Modern Japan.* Cambridge: Harvard University Press, 1995.

Ishii Susumu, *Nihon no rekishi 12: Chūsei bushidan.* Tokyo: Shōgakkan, 1974.

Martin, Joel, "The Samurai Crab." *Terra,* vol. 31, no. 4 (1991).

McCullough, Helen Craig, transl. and intro., *The Tale of the Heike.* Stanford: Stanford University Press, 1988.

Nihon Kokugo Daijiten Dai ni-han Henshū Iinkai, Shōgakkan Kokugo Jiten Henshūbu, eds., *Nihon kokugo daijiten.* Tokyo: Shōgakkan, 2000–2002.

Rath, Eric C., *Food and Fantasy in Early Modern Japan.* Berkeley: University of California Press, 2010.

Saitō Tsutomu, *Kinzoku ga kataru Nihon shi: senka, nihontō, teppō.* Tokyo: Yoshikawa Kōbunkan, 2012.

Selinger, Vyjayanthi R., *Authorizing the Shogunate: Ritual and Material Symbolism in the Literary Construction of Warrior Order.* Leiden: Brill, 2013.

Souyri, Pierre, *The World Turned Upside Down: Medieval Japanese Society.* New York: Columbia University Press, 2001.

Tsang, Carol R., *War and Faith: Ikkō Ikki in Late Muromachi Japan.* Cambridge: Harvard University Asia Center, 2007.

Chapter 3
The Art and Science of the Sword

Cooper, Michael, *They Came to Japan: An Anthology of European Reports, 1543–1640.* Berkeley: University of California Press, 1965. (Quotation from Alessandro Valignano).

Howland, Douglas, *Borders of Chinese Civilization: Geography and History at Empire's End.* Durham, NC: Duke University Press, 1996.

Ikegami, Eiko, *The Taming of the Samurai: Honorific Individualism and the Making of Modern Japan.* Cambridge: Harvard University Press, 1995.

Mills, D. E., "Kataki-uchi: The Practice of Blood-Revenge in Pre-Modern Japan." *Modern Asian Studies,* vol. 10, no. 4 (1976).

Ogawa, Morihiro, ed., *Art of the Samurai: Japanese Arms and Armor, 1156–1868.* New York: The Metropolitan Museum of Art, 2009.

Parker, C. K. and S. Morisawa, trans., "Kokaji: A Nō Play in Two Acts." *Monumenta Nipponica,* vol. 3, no. 2 (July 1940), p. 619–629.

Pitelka, Morgan, "Review of Morihiro Ogawa, ed., *Art of the Samurai,*" *Japanese Studies* vol. 30, no. 3 (2010).

— "Should Museums Welcome Parody?" *Early Modern Japan* 19 (2011).

— "The Tokugawa Storehouse: Ieyasu's Encounters with Things," in Paula Findlen, ed., *Early Modern Things: Objects and their Histories, 1500–1800.* New York: Routledge, 2012.

Smith, Henry D. II., "Review of *Lords of the Samurai: Legacy of a Daimyo Family* by Yoko Woodson, *Art of the Samurai: Selections from the Tokyo National Museum* by Kazutoshi Harada, and *Art of the Samurai: Japanese Arms and Armor, 1156–1868* by Morihiro Ogawa," *CAA Reviews* (2012).

Weins, William N. and Peter Bleed, "Why Is the Japanese Sword Curved?" in Vandiver, Pamela B., James R. Druzik, and George S. Wheeler, et al., *Materials Issues in Art and Archaeology II: Symposium Held April 17–21, 1990, San Francisco, California, USA. Materials Research Society Symposium Series,* vol. 185. Pittsburgh: Materials Research Society, 1991.

Chapter 4
Edo and the Architecture
of the Great Peace

Coaldrake, William H., "Metaphors of the Metropolis: Architectural and Artistic Representations of the Identity of Edo," in Nicolas Fiévé and Paul Waley, eds., *Japanese Capitals in Historical Perspective: Place, Power and Memory in Kyoto, Edo and Tokyo.* New York: RoutledgeCurzon, 2003.

Kokusho Kankōkai, eds., "Kanbun inchi-shū." *Zokuzoku gunsho ruijū 9 chiri-bu.* Tokyo: Kokuritsu Shiryōkan, 1978.

Nishioka Toranosuke and Hattori Shisō, eds., *Nihon rekishi chizu.* Tokyo: Zenkoku Kyōiku Tosho, 1956.

Parker, Geoffrey, *Global Crisis: War, Climate Change and Catastrophe in the Seventeenth Century.* New Haven: Yale University Press, 2013.

Roberts, Luke S., *Performing the Great Peace: Political Space and Open Secrets in Tokugawa Japan.* Honolulu: University of Hawai'i Press, 2012.

Suitō Makoto and Katō Takashi, eds., *Edo-zu byōbu wo yomu.* Tokyo: Tōkyōdō Shuppan, 2000.

Toby, Ronald P., *State and Diplomacy in Early Modern Japan: Asia in the Development of the Tokugawa Bakufu.* Princeton: Princeton University Press, 1984.

Vaporis, Constantine Nomikos, *Tour of Duty: Samurai, Military Service in Edo, and the Culture of Early Modern Japan.* Honolulu: University of Hawai'i Press, 2008.

Walthall, Anne, "Hiding the Shoguns: Secrecy and the Nature of Political Authority in Tokugawa Japan," in Bernhard Scheid and Mark Teeuwen, eds., *The Culture of Secrecy in Japanese Religion.* New York: Routledge, 2006.

Yoshino Tomio, "Ainu no aizō seru shikki nit suite." *Bijutsu kenkyū,* vol. 64 (1937).

Chapter 5
Armament or Ornament?

Asakawa Kan'ichi, "Bushidō." Typewritten manuscript for a public lecture, Kan'ichi Asakawa Papers (MS 40). Manuscripts and Archives, Yale University Library. Published in Yabuki Susumu, ed., *Asakawa Kan'ichi hikaku hōkensei ronshū*. Tokyo: Kashiwa Shobō, 2007.

Friday, Karl F., *Samurai, Warfare and the State in Early Medieval Japan*. Honolulu: University of Hawai'i Press, 2004.

Muscarella, Frank and Michael R. Cunningham, "The Evolutionary Significance and Social Perception of Male Pattern Baldness and Facial Hair." *Ethology and Sociobiology*, vol. 17 (1996).

Ogawa, Morihiro, ed., *Art of the Samurai: Japanese Arms and Armor, 1156–1868*. New York: The Metropolitan Museum of Art, 2009.

Pitelka, Morgan, "Review of Morihiro Ogawa, ed., *Art of the Samurai.*" *Japanese Studies*, vol. 30, no. 3 (2010).

—"Should Museums Welcome Parody?" *Early Modern Japan*, vol. 19 (2011).

Smith, Henry D. II., "Review of Yoko Woodson, *Lords of the Samurai*, Kazutoshi Harada, ed., *Art of the Samurai*, and Morihiro Ogawa, ed., *Art of the Samurai.*" *CAA Reviews* (2012).

Suga, Takaaki, "Perceptions of Edo-period Armor." *Bulletin of the Detroit Museum of Art*, vol. 88, no. 1/4 (2014).

Yamakawa Kikue and Kate Wildman Nakai, transl. and intro., *Women of the Mito Domain: Recollections of Samurai Family Life*. Tokyo: Tokyo University Press, 1992.

Chapter 6
Samurai Aesthetics:
Extravagance and Restraint

Berry, Mary Elizabeth, *The Culture of Civil War in Kyoto*. Berkeley: University of California Press, 1994.

Cooper, Michael, *They Came to Japan: An Anthology of European Reports, 1543–1640*. Berkeley: University of California Press, 1965. (Quoted passages from Alessandro Valignano, Luis de Almeida, and João Rodrigues).

Inumura Tadashi and Yoshida Mitsukuni, eds., *The Traditional Crafts of Japan 4 Lacquerware*. Tokyo: Diamond, 1992.

Ohki, Sadaki, *Tea Culture of Japan*. New Haven: Yale University Art Gallery, 2009.

Ortolani, Benito, *The Japanese Theatre: From Shamanistic Ritual to Contemporary Pluralism*. Rev. ed. Princeton: Princeton University Press, 1995.

Pitelka, Morgan, ed., *Japanese Tea Culture: Art, History, and Practice*. New York: Routledge, 2003.

Stalker, John and George Parker, *A Treatise of Japanning and Varnishing*. Oxford: Printed for, and sold by, the author, at Mr. Richard Wood's house over against the Theater in Oxford, 1688.

Staples, Loretta N., *A Sense of Pattern: Textile Masterworks from the Yale University Art Gallery*. New Haven: Yale University Press, 1981.

Tanizaki Jun'ichirō, *In'ei raisan*. Tokyo: Chūō kōronsha, 1995. (Originally 1933).

Yonemura, Ann, "Splendour and Supremacy: Lacquer for the Tokugawa," in Musée des beaux-arts de Montréal, and Tokugawa Bijutsukan, eds., *The Japan of the Shoguns*. Montreal: The Montreal Museum of Fine Arts, 1989.

Yotsuyanagi Kashō, *Urushi no bunkashi*. Tokyo: Iwanami Shoten, 2009.

Chapter 7
The Samurai Imagined

Izzard, Sebastian, *Kunisada's World*. New York: Japan Society, 1993.

Katsumori Noriko, "Tairō kara Kuniyoshi he: bijutsu ni miru ransho juyō no katachi." *Kōbe shiritsu hakubutsukan kenkyū kiyō*, vol. 16 (March 2000), p. 17–44.

Keene, Donald, trans., *Chūshingura: The Treasury of Loyal Retainers*. New York: Columbia University Press, 1971.

Kikuchi Yōsuke, "Jitsuroku to ehon yomihon: Hayami Shungyōsai gasaku 'jitsuroku-shu' ehon yomihon wo megutte." *Kinsei bungei*, vol. 86 (July 2007), p. 41–55.

Knox, Katharine McCook, *Surprise Personalities in Georgetown, D.C.* [Washington, D.C.]: [W. Lynnwood Cook, Service Printing Co.], 1958.

Kornicki, Peter, *The Book in Japan: A Cultural History from the Beginnings to the Nineteenth Century*. Honolulu: University of Hawai'i Press, 2001.

Saito, Shiuichiro and Edward Greey, trans., *The Loyal Ronins: An Historical Romance, Translated from the Japanese*. New York: G. P. Putnam's Sons, 1880.

Shively, Donald, "Bakufu Versus Kabuki." *Harvard Journal of Asiatic Studies*, vol. 18, no. 3/4 (December 1955), p. 326–356.

Chapter 8
Death and the Good Life

Kaempfer, Engelbert and Beatrice Bodard-Bailey, ed., transl., and ann., *Kaempfer's Japan: Tokugawa Culture Observed*. Honolulu: University of Hawai'i, 1999.

Drixler, Fabian F., *Mabiki: Infanticide and Population Growth in Eastern Japan, 1660–1950*. Berkeley: University of California Press, 1994.

Hur, Nam-lin, *Death and Social Order in Tokugawa Japan: Buddhism, Anti-Christianity, and the Danka System*. Cambridge: Harvard University Asia Center, 2007.

Chapter 9
Forbidden Waters
and Foreign Knowledge

Boxer, C. R., *The Christian Century in Japan, 1549–1650*. Berkeley: University of California Press, 1967.

Elman, Benjamin A., "Sinophiles and Sinophobes in Tokugawa Japan: Politics, Classicism, and Medicine during the Eighteenth Century." in *East Asian Science, Technology and Society*, vol. 2 (2008), p. 93–121.

Hur, Nam-lin, *Death and Social Order in Tokugawa Japan: Buddhism, Anti-Christianity, and the Danka System*. Cambridge: Harvard University Asia Center, 2007.

Laver, Michael S., *The Sakoku Edicts and the Politics of Tokugawa Hegemony*. Amherst, NY: Cambria Press, 2011.

Keene, Donald, *The Japanese Discovery of Europe, 1720–1830*. Stanford: Stanford University Press, 1969.

Matsuzaki, Akitomo, *Seishu Hanaoka and His Medicine: A Japanese Pioneer of Anesthesia and Surgery*. Hirosaki: Hirosaki University Press, 2011.

Screech, Timon, *The Lens within the Heart: The Western Scientific Gaze and Popular Imagery in Later Edo Japan*. Honolulu: University of Hawai'i Press, 2002.

Toby, Ronald P., *State and Diplomacy in Early Modern Japan: Asia in the Development of the Tokugawa Bakufu*. Princeton: Princeton University Press, 1984.

Chapter 10
Japan in Ainu Lands

Akino, Shigeki, "Spirit-Sending Ceremonies," in William W. Fitzhugh and Chisato O. Dubreuil, eds., *Ainu: Spirit of a Northern People*. Washington, DC: Arctic Studies Center, National Museum of Natural History, Smithsonian Institution, in association with University of Washington Press, 1999.

Benfey, Christopher, *The Great Wave: Gilded Age Misfits, Japanese Eccentrics, and the Opening of Old Japan*. New York: Random House, 2003.

Dubreuil, Chisato O., "Ainu Art: the Beginnings of Tradition," in William W. Fitzhugh and Chisato O. Dubreuil, eds., *Ainu: Spirit of a Northern People.* Washington, DC: Arctic Studies Center, National Museum of Natural History, Smithsonian Institution, in association with University of Washington Press, 1999.

Fujimura, Hisakazu, "Life and Death," in William W. Fitzhugh and Chisato O. Dubreuil, eds., *Ainu: Spirit of a Northern People.* Washington, DC: Arctic Studies Center, National Museum of Natural History, Smithsonian Institution, in association with University of Washington Press, 1999.

Henning, Joseph M., *Outposts of Civilization: Race, Religion, and the Formative Years of American–Japanese Relations.* New York: New York University Press, 2000.

Howell, David L., *Capitalism from Within: Economy, Society, and the State in a Japanese Fishery.* Berkeley: University of California Press, 1995.

Howell, David L., "The Ainu and the Early Modern Japanese State, 1600–1868," in William W. Fitzhugh and Chisato O. Dubreuil, eds., *Ainu: Spirit of a Northern People.* Washington, DC: Arctic Studies Center, National Museum of Natural History, Smithsonian Institution in association with University of Washington Press, 1999.

Kayano Shigeru, *Ainu no mingu.* Tokyo: Suzusawa Shoten, 1978.

Keira, Mitsunori and Tomoko Keira, "Village Work: Gender Roles and Seasonal Work," in William W. Fitzhugh and Chisato O. Dubreuil, eds., *Ainu: Spirit of a Northern People.* Washington, DC: Arctic Studies Center, National Museum of Natural History, Smithsonian Institution, in association with University of Washington Press, 1999.

Kikuchi, Isao, "Early Ainu Contacts with the Japanese," in William W. Fitzhugh and Chisato O. Dubreuil, eds., *Ainu: Spirit of a Northern People.* Washington, DC: Arctic Studies Center, National Museum of Natural History, Smithsonian Institution, in association with University of Washington Press, 1999.

Kindaichi Kyōsuke and Sugiyama Sueo, *Ainu geijutsu.* Sapporo: Hokkaidō Shuppan Kikaku Sentā, 1973.

Kodama, Mari, "Clothing and Ornamentation," in William W. Fitzhugh and Chisato O. Dubreuil, eds., *Ainu: Spirit of a Northern People.* Washington, DC: Arctic Studies Center, National Museum of Natural History, Smithsonian Institution, in association

with University of Washington Press, 1999.

Kotani, Yoshinobu, "Ainu Collections in North America: Documentation Projects and the Frederick Starr Collections," in William W. Fitzhugh and Chisato O. Dubreuil, eds., *Ainu: Spirit of a Northern People.* Washington, DC: Arctic Studies Center, National Museum of Natural History, Smithsonian Institution, in association with University of Washington Press, 1999.

Landor, Arnold Henry Savage, *Alone with the Hairy Ainu. Or, 3800 Miles on a Pack Saddle in Yezo and a Cruise to the Kurile Islands.* London: J. Murray, 1893.

Maraini, Fosco, "*Ikupasuy*: It's Not a Moustache Lifter!" in William W. Fitzhugh and Chisato O. Dubreuil, eds., *Ainu: Spirit of a Northern People.* Washington, DC: Arctic Studies Center, National Museum of Natural History, Smithsonian Institution, in association with University of Washington Press, 1999.

Murakami Shimanojō, *Ezotō kikan.* Manuscript, 1799. Tokyo National Museum.

Refsing, Kirsten, *Early European Writings on Ainu Culture.* Richmond, Surrey: Curzon, 2000.

Sasaki, Toshikazu, "Ainu-e: A Historical Review," in William W. Fitzhugh and Chisato O. Dubreuil, eds., *Ainu: Spirit of a Northern People.* Washington, DC: Arctic Studies Center, National Museum of Natural History, Smithsonian Institution, in association with University of Washington Press, 1999.

Yang, Sunny and Rochelle N. Narasin, *Textile Art of Japan.* Tokyo: Shufunotomo, 1989.

Yoshino Tomio, "Ainu no aizō seru shikki nit suite." *Bijitsu kenkyū,* vol. 64 (1937).

Yotsuyanagi Kashō, *Urushi no bunkashi.* Tokyo: Iwanami Shoten, 2009.

Chapter 11
The Opening of Japan, the Closing of the Great Peace

Benfey, Christopher E. G., *The Great Wave: Gilded Age Misfits, Japanese Eccentrics, and the Opening of Old Japan.* New York: Random House, 2003.

Davis, Lance E., Robert E. Gallman, and Karin Gleiter, *In Pursuit of Leviathan: Technology, Institutions, Productivity, and Profits in American Whaling, 1816–1906.* Chicago: University of Chicago Press, 2007.

Howell, David L., "Foreign Encounters and Informal Diplomacy in Early

Modern Japan." *Journal of Japanese Studies,* vol. 40, no. 2 (2014).

Jansen, Marius B., *The Making of Modern Japan.* Cambridge: Harvard University Press, 2002.

Jones, Ryan T., *Empire of Extinction: Russians and the North Pacific's Strange Beasts of the Sea, 1741–1867.* New York: Oxford University Press, 2014.

Keene, Donald, *Emperor of Japan: Meiji and His World, 1852–1912.* New York: Columbia University Press, 2002.

Lensen, George A., *The Russian Push Toward Japan: Russo-Japanese Relations, 1697–1875.* Princeton: Princeton University Press, 1959.

Ravina, Mark, *The Last Samurai: The Life and Battles of Saigo Takamori.* Hoboken, NJ: Wiley, 2003.

Richards, John F., *The World Hunt: an Environmental History of the Commodification of Animals.* Berkeley: University of California Press, 2014.

Smith, Thomas C., "Japan's Aristocratic Revolution." *Yale Review,* vol. 50, no. 3 (1961).

Smith, Tim D., Randall R. Reeves, Elizabeth A. Josephson, and Judith N. Lund, "Spatial and Seasonal Distribution of American Whaling and Whales in the Age of Sail." *PLoS ONE,* vol. 7, no. 4 (2012).

Steele, M. William, *Alternative Narratives of Modern Japanese History.* London: Routledge, 2003.

The Yale Collectors

Gregory, Herbert E., Report of the Director for 1925. *Bernice P. Bishop Museum Bulletin,* vol. 28. Honolulu: Bernice P. Bishop Museum, 1926.

Guth, Christine M. E., "The Formation of the Japanese Collections in the Peabody Essex Museum." *Orientations,* vol. 32, no. 5 (May 2001), p. 67–73.

Hammond, Ellen H., "A History of the East Asia Library at Yale University" in Peter X. Zhou, ed., *Collecting Asia: East Asian Libraries in North America, 1868–2008.* Ann Arbor: Association for Asian Studies, 2010, p. 3–20.

Mabel Loomis Todd Letters. Archives of the Peabody Essex Museum.

Sewall, Richard B., *The Life of Emily Dickinson.* New York: Farrar, Strauss and Giroux, 1974.

Shepherd Stevens Papers (MS 865). Manuscripts and Archives, Yale University Library.

Todd, Mabel Loomis, *Corona and Coronet.* New York: Houghton, Mifflin and Company, 1899.

Index